SKIING FIT

THE FITNESS GUIDE
SPECIFICALLY
DESIGNED FOR SKIERS

STAN PALMER

The Crowood Press

First published in 1989 by
The Crowood Press
Ramsbury, Marlborough,
Wiltshire SN8 2HE

British Library Cataloguing in Publication Data

Palmer, Stan
  Skiing fit.
  1. Skiers. Physical fitness. Exercises
  I. Title
  613.7'1

  ISBN 1 85223 126 2

Photographs by David Peters
Line-Drawings by Janet Sparrow

Typeset by Griffin & Reiver, Gloucester
Printed in Great Britain by The Bath Press

Contents

Foreword

Stan Palmer's 'right to write' on fitness is based on a background of personal performance, high-level coaching and many years of experience and research. An excellent all-round sportsman, teacher and coach, his lectures and writing on sports structures, sports philosophy and mental and physical readiness for performance are nationally recognised.

Many governing bodies of sport, not least my own, use Stan Palmer in their coach education programmes at all levels. Stan's original mind analysed that if true potential at any level in any sport were to be achieved, then a child must experience a proper foundation period in terms of physical development, co-ordination and control. He recognised that hard physical preparation was necessary if satisfactory skill acquisition was to be achieved.

Everyone can enjoy skiing if they follow this book's carefully structured programmes and targets. Baden-Powell in setting his philosophy for the Scouting Movement crystallised it in the motto 'Be prepared'.

Stan Palmer is ensuring that if we structure our year properly we can be fully prepared for a wonderful winter sports experience. We will know more about ourselves – physically and mentally. We will have tested ourselves and enjoyed noting our progress. Accompanying our improved physical condition and physical awareness will be a new mental security and control which will ensure our success on 'the slopes' and contribute to a new physical and mental well-being.

Robert Burns' statement, 'Would that God the gift would give us to see ourselves as others see us!', will always apply but Stan Palmer's wisdom if noted will give us all a chance to reflect that perhaps it was not the instructor, the hotel, the airline or the courier that was at fault – it was us. We have time left so let us enjoy applying to ourselves the message of this excellent book.

J. Atkinson MBE
Technical Director
British Amateur Gymnastics Association

Introduction

The skiers returning from their holidays who have not made the improvement and progress they hoped for apportion blame to a long list of possible causes. They include their skis and boots, the weather, the snow conditions, the hotel, the food – even the tour operator and the airline are not safe from unjustified criticism – but it is usually their instructor who has to shoulder most of the blame. It is, of course, possible to be allocated to a group where an instructor is apparently not interested or is genuinely unable to do his job but such instructors are, in all fairness, a very small minority. Providing the instructor holds the appropriate qualifications, teaching is comparatively easy. It is learning that is difficult, and the ability to learn can be attributed only to the skiers themselves.

The majority of the recreational skiers who regularly watch *Ski Sunday* would have very little sympathy with Pirmin Zubriggen, Peter Mueller or Martin Bell if they failed to achieve their best because they were not fit enough for competition. There is an accepted link between fitness and performance for all the top sportsmen and women. What is harder to accept is that there is a proven link between fitness and performance at all levels of ability and aspiration.

Most recreational skiers approach the preparations for their skiing holiday in the same casual manner as they do a holiday on the beach where gentle bathing is the most strenuous activity. As a result, ski instructors all over the world are confronted with clients who are physically unable to do what is asked of them. Without mobility of the hips even a simple kick turn is at best difficult. Many find the unaccustomed exercise extremely tiring. Little wonder as the energy expenditure in a week's skiing may be the equivalent of swimming the Channel.

While there is an obvious speed difference between racers and recreational skiers there is very little difference in the requirements of the muscles for their respective techniques. Similarly, residual muscle soreness and stiffness strike without discrimination racers and recreational skiers who ignore the need for mobility of the muscles and joints.

Fortunately, fatal accidents are fewer in skiing than in any other of the hazardous pursuits: canoeing, caving, climbing and sailing. But in contrast there are more skiing accidents that require medical attention than in the combined total of all the other activities. Skiing accidents are viewed as a source of some amusement and accepted with an air of inevitability that is absurd and their severity could be dramatically reduced if much greater attention was given to fitness prior to participation. The most important factor in avoiding injury is fitness.

Ignoring the need for fitness prior to departure to the snow or the artificial slope facility is an expensive mistake – not only in financial terms but also in the loss of self-satisfaction that comes from not making the progress for which one had hoped.

1 What is Fitness?

Before considering how fitness may be improved, it is sensible to look at what fitness is and, equally important, what it is not.

Because fitness and health are closely related and interdependent they are frequently thought to be the same thing. In fact in the context of sport and performance each has distinct characteristics.

Health is the condition of a person in respect of illness and disease. All health-related problems should be dealt with by doctors. Fitness may be dealt with by coaches, trainers, physiotherapists, the performers themselves and, in cases of acute injury, sports medical specialists.

Good health is essential before commencing and for continuing with any fitness training programme that places stress on an individual. Consequently, a thorough health check-up is recommended for all over-40s, and those with sedentary occupations who do not regularly participate in an active recreation, before they start a fit-to-ski training programme. Good health should be viewed as a prerequisite to fitness, just as fitness must be seen as a prerequisite to learning to ski and improving performance.

Fitness is the readiness of an individual to learn and accurately perform sports techniques. The exact nature of the requirements is determined by the techniques of the sport and the environment in which they are performed. Not surprisingly, then, fitness for skiing is quite different from that for badminton, cricket, soccer and all the traditional lowland games. The movement patterns of skiing and the 'playing surface' are so alien to what is normal that the need to prepare the body to learn should be readily accepted.

Fitness is frequently represented as being simple, easy to attain and consisting only of stamina, mobility and muscular strength. In fact it is complex, difficult to attain yet comparatively easy to maintain and consists of a number of components. A complete list should include: agility, balance, body build, confidence, courage, health, posture, mental fitness, mobility, muscular endurance, muscular power, muscular strength, and stamina.

The importance of each component is dependent on the nature of the sport. In shot-putting, for example, body build and strength are the most important. Nordic skiers and marathon runners rely mainly on stamina and muscular endurance. In badminton hand–eye co-ordination, agility, stamina and muscular endurance are the keys.

For recreational skiers learning and performance must be viewed as two separate but equally important requirements. Learning the techniques correctly and being able to perform a limited number is dependent on agility, balance, confidence, mobility, muscular power, and a correct posture. To repeat the techniques in a skilful manner during a day's skiing requires, in addition, stamina and muscular endurance.

Another common but inaccurate view of fitness is that it is improved or even obtained by participation in an activity. Those who follow this advice are likely to experience some difficulty in learning the techniques correctly and will find that their progress is limited. If, for example, the muscles that should be making the movements are not in a suitable condition, others will be utilised with the result that the techniques are learned incorrectly. Similarly, those who try to improve their stamina by participation in skiing are much more likely to be involved in an accident when skill breaks down as a result of fatigue than those who improve their stamina before they ski.

Fitness should be improved prior to participation. This is emphasised in what is perhaps the most accurate definition of sports fitness: 'in a suitable condition or ready for . . .' As well as emphasising the need to prepare for participation, this definition also points to the fact that fitness is specific to each activity. Someone who is fit to play football or tennis should not assume that they are also fit to ski.

HEALTH CARE

A commonsense approach to health care is very important. Good health has already been emphasised as a prerequisite to fitness. There is more than a grain of truth in the statement, 'Fitness training can damage your health.' Certainly training that imposes even controlled stress on the physiological systems can, if a person is unhealthy, cause a worsening of their condition. This is particularly true of viral infections, where training increases body temperature.

The importance of a thorough health check-up before a training programme is started cannot be overemphasised, especially for those who are not normally active and who may have sedentary occupations.

Similarly it is necessary to interrupt a training programme to consult a doctor as soon as a health problem occurs in order to minimise the risk of aggravating the condition.

A healthier life-style is the first phase in any programme designed to improve fitness.

Alcohol and Tobacco

The detrimental effects of both alcohol and tobacco on one's health are extremely well known and publicised. Anyone considering improving their ski fitness must realise that the task will be made extremely difficult by both products. Reducing alcohol consumption to reasonable levels and stopping smoking will improve one's health and make the road to fitness easier to follow.

Body-Weight

The mastery of sports techniques is in part determined by body build and body shape. It is important to realise that, just as there is an ideal shape and weight for high-jumpers, shot-putters and gymnasts, so one's ability to learn to ski is also determined by body type. People with a heavy or large frame and those of medium and light frames who are overweight find themselves at a distinct disadvantage. Agility is an essential element of ski technique and it is inhibited by being overweight.

Fitness training places a controlled stress on an individual in order to obtain an adaptation to the new workloads. Being overweight can place an intolerable stress on the heart if the training is at all energetic and instead of bringing about an improvement in fitness can cause a deterioration in one's health.

Nothing can be done to alter bone structure. That is determined by genetics. Being overweight can also be something that is passed from one generation to the next. However, it is usually possible to reduce weight by dieting. While there are numerous and probably successful commercial systems available at varying costs, it is preferable for those who intend to tackle the problem of excess weight to consult their doctor.

Nutrition

A correct and varied diet is necessary if the human body is to be able to work at its maximum efficiency. It is a complex mechanism dependent on adequate supplies of the correct foods to provide fuel for energy and nutrients for recovery and growth. Each individual's dietary requirements are dependent on their age, sex, body build, daily routine and the rate at which they consume the fuel.

The average person's normal consumption ensures that there are adequate supplies to build new tissues, to repair worn out and damaged parts and also to provide a source of energy for activity. A varied diet should provide carbohydrates, fats, minerals, protein, water and vitamins. If the daily diet of those in a fitness programme includes the following, it is unlikely that a deficiency will occur:

Meat, eggs	1 daily portion
Milk, cheese, yoghurt	2 daily portions
Poultry, fish	1 daily portion
Vegetables, fruit	3 daily portions
Wholemeal bread, pasta, rice	3 daily portions
Butter, margarine	25g (1oz)

As the body is able to store nutrients, it is most unlikely that any short-term deficiency will adversely affect either training or performance. Reserves will be utilised and replenished when a normal varied diet is resumed.

The one exception concerns the intake of fluids. Exercise causes the body to lose water and salt. Even quite small losses can bring about an impairment of muscular performance. It is essential therefore to ensure adequate intake of liquid before and during exercise.

The Prevention and Treatment of Injuries

As it is most unlikely that injury can always be avoided, advice on how the incidence may be reduced and on what to do following an injury is beneficial.

Certainly prevention must be considered better than cure. All training must be planned having taken into account the trainee's age and level of fitness at the start of the training programme. The initial workloads and the targets for improvement must be realistic and within comparatively easy reach.

Training injuries are reduced if the facets of fitness are improved in the following order:

(1) mobility
(2) posture
(3) stamina and muscular endurance
(4) power and strength

A thorough warm-up should precede all training sessions. The clothing and footwear should be appropriate for the activity. Special care must be taken in the choice of training shoes. Those with hard, high backs can exert pressure and damage the Achilles

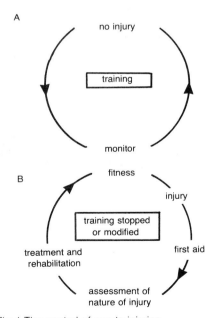

Fig 1 The control of sports injuries.

tendon. Runners and joggers who train on the roads must have shoes with a well-cushioned sole to minimise the effects of the jarring as the foot contacts the running surface.

Whatever type of exercise is employed, it is vitally important that the joints are moved through their full range of movement.

The correct pattern of movement for each and every exercise must be learned and practised before the exercise is performed in a pressure training situation.

An overview of the recommended system for the prevention and treatment of all injuries is perhaps most easily understood with reference to Fig 1.

While there are no problems training is continued and fitness monitored by regular testing.

This pattern is interrupted as soon as an injury occurs. Pain is an indicator that all is not well. It must not be ignored because what might be a comparatively minor problem can easily be aggravated and made more serious by continuing training.

The normal and sensible practice, as indicated in the diagram, is to administer first aid as soon as possible and thereby reduce the extent of the injury. It will vary from the application of an ice pack to minor bruises and strains to the immobilisation of limbs where fractures are suspected. Any first aid, however, must be entirely dependent on the knowledge of the person giving the help. Far too often people with no real knowledge of first aid administer 'help' that has been described by Dr. Thomas as 'Largely unqualified, usually idiosyncratic and frequently harmful'. Dr. Williams observes how 'Too often sportsmen, when injured, are handled on the spot by well-meaning but ill-informed people who make the injury far worse than it could be'. The temptation to role-play and act knowledgeable must be resisted. 'The untrained person can best serve the victim by getting proper help.'

The next stage following first aid, assuming injury merits it, is to obtain a diagnosis of the exact nature of the injury. This unfortunately can be difficult. Many general practitioners appear not to be oversympathetic towards injured sportsmen unless the injury is perceived by them to be serious. While the number of sports injury clinics is slowly increasing and diagnosis and treatment are more accessible in some areas, Dr Reilly's statement is still accurate: 'Sports medical specialists are identified by their great scarcity and by their difficulty of access to sportsmen.'

Nevertheless some advice and guidance should, if possible, be obtained, treatment of the injury started and a programme of rehabilitation established. Dr Maddox recommends the resumption of training only when the following recovery is attained:

- 80 per cent of normal range of movement
- 50 per cent of normal power
- less than 20 per cent of original swelling
- normal stability of the joint
- no pain at rest

2 Improving Fitness

Improving fitness is a long-term process. It cannot be achieved in four weeks, in five minutes a day or in an hour a week as some claim. Obviously the length of time it takes is partially dependent on the level of fitness before a training programme is started and the amount of time that is devoted to training. The most unfit will notice the most immediate improvement but will have the longest road to travel.

The effectiveness of any training programme is dependent on it being tailored to meet the needs of each individual, whose strengths and weaknesses have been determined by fitness tests.

The following test battery seeks to test the facets of fitness which are known to correlate with ski ability.

Mobility 1   Straddle Sit/Reach

Sit on the floor, legs straight and at right angles. (Sitting at the corner of a mat will ensure that the legs are in the correct position.) Place a garden cane or straight stick joining the soles of the feet. Reach as far forward as possible. Measure the distance that can be reached beyond the cane.

Mobility 2   Straight Leg Reach

Sit on the floor, legs straight and knees and ankles together. Slide the hands along the floor and reach as far as possible. Record the distance reached past the soles of the feet.

Power 1   Sargent Jump

Stand facing a wall, toes touching the wall. Reach up with both hands and make a mark on the wall with the fingertips at full-stretch height. (Use chalk, eye shadow, soot, etc. to make the mark.) Turn sideways to stand facing along the wall, 30–45 cms from the wall. Bend the legs, spring up and make a second mark on the wall with the hand nearest to the wall. Measure and record the distance between the first and second marks.

Power 2   Box Jumps

Place an empty crisp box on a non-slip floor. Mark a line on the floor 30 cm from both sides of the box. Stand to one side of the box then, taking off and landing on two feet, jump over the box and back. Do as many as possible in one minute. Count one each time both feet touch the floor.

Strength   Leg Bends

Stand on one leg (a chair back or table may be used for balance). Bend the knee to 45°, then straighten the leg and lift the heel. Do as many as possible in one minute.

Posture

Sit on the floor, legs straight. Keeping heels on the floor, lean back to 45° and hold as long as possible.

Stamina

This is the only test that cannot be done at home. A 400-metre track is required. The test is to run, jog or walk as far as possible in 12 minutes.

The tests need not all be conducted on the

Fig 2 Mobility: straddle sit.

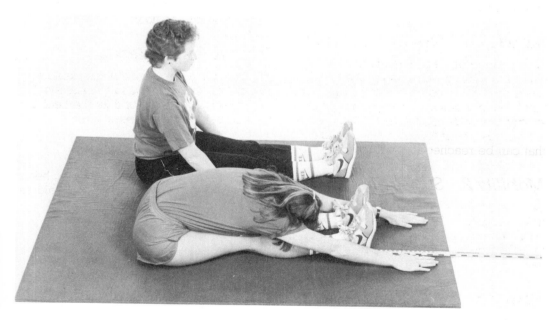

Fig 3 Mobility: straight leg reach.

Fig 4 Power: sargent jump.

Fig 5 Power: box jumps.

Fig 6 Strength: leg bends.

Fig 7 Posture: sit/lean back.

	Target	Test	Target	Test	Target	Test	Target	Test
Mobility								
1. Straddle sit	✓	7	12	11	16	17		
2. Straight legs	/	3	5	6	8	8		
Power								
1. Sargent jump	/	21	25	27	30	29		
2. Box jumps	/	47	60	62	65	67		
Posture								
Sit/lean back	/	17	25	28	35	36		
Strength								
Leg bends	/	41	50	46	50	51		
Stamina								
12-minute run	/	1,150	1,300	1,275	1,350	1,375		

Fig 8 Fitness test: record chart.

	Excellent	Good	Average	Poor	Very Weak	
	5	4	3	2	1	0
Mobility 1. Straddle sit	35cm	25	20	15	10	<10
2. Straight leg	25cm	20	15	10	5	<5
Power 1. Sargent jump	50	40	30	25	20	<20
2. Box jump	70	60	50	40	30	<30
Strength Leg bends (right) Leg bends (left)	50	40	30	20	15	<15
Posture Sit/lean back	40 secs	35	30	25	20	<20
Stamina 12-minute run	2,800m	2,400	2,000	1,600	1,200	<1,200

Fig 9 Fitness test scores.

same day but should if possible all be completed within a week.

The results should be recorded on a record card (see Fig 8). This record should be used to monitor progress. This will be a source of motivation to continue when, as will happen from time to time, the desire to continue may decline. It may also be used to record realistic, realisable targets for improvement for the next test session.

With the exception of the 12-minute stamina test, it is recommended that tests are conducted at 4–6-week intervals. A more realistic interval for the stamina test is 10–12 weeks. Testing more frequently does not allow sufficient time for improvement and this may create a negative attitude to training.

PLANNING A FITNESS PROGRAMME

There are two important considerations when planning a fitness training programme: what needs to be done; and what time is regularly available for training.

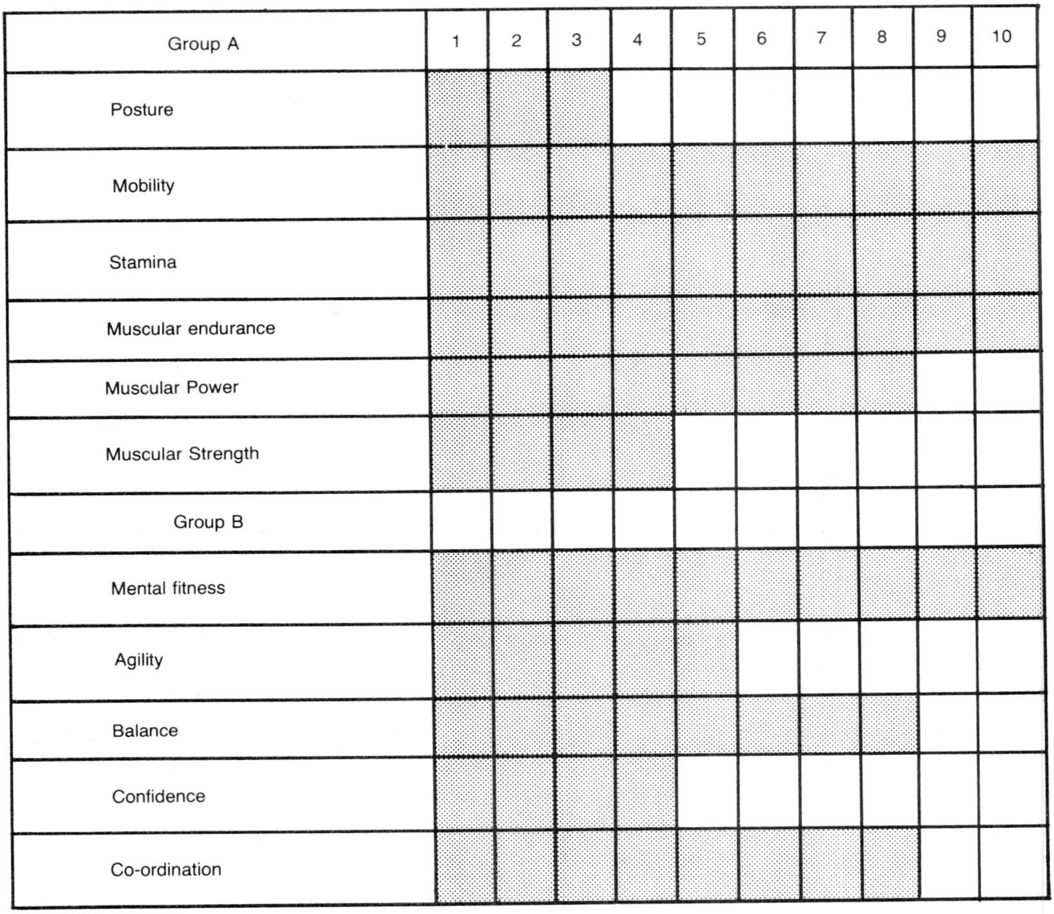

Group A	1	2	3	4	5	6	7	8	9	10
Posture										
Mobility										
Stamina										
Muscular endurance										
Muscular Power										
Muscular Strength										
Group B										
Mental fitness										
Agility										
Balance										
Confidence										
Co-ordination										

Fig 10 Alpine recreational fitness profile.

What needs to be improved is determined by the specific requirements of the sport. This is termed a *sport profile*.

Having completed the fitness tests, each individual should compare his or her current status with that required by the recreational skier's profile. The priority must be to improve all those facets where the test score achieved was average – 3 or less. There is no point spending hours jogging or cycling to improve stamina if that is already at an acceptable level and the time could be used to better effect improving mobility, for example.

The profile shows two distinct groups of fitness components. Group A are most easily improved 'off skis' prior to participation. Group B are most easily improved 'on skis' as part of the process of learning to ski. It is extremely doubtful that any 'off ski' training of agility, balance, courage/confidence and kinaesthesis will transfer and have any positive effect on an adult's performance on skis.

The second phase of planning a fitness training programme is to decide when training will take place. Unless a training timetable is produced and adhered to, there is a strong possibility that very little will be

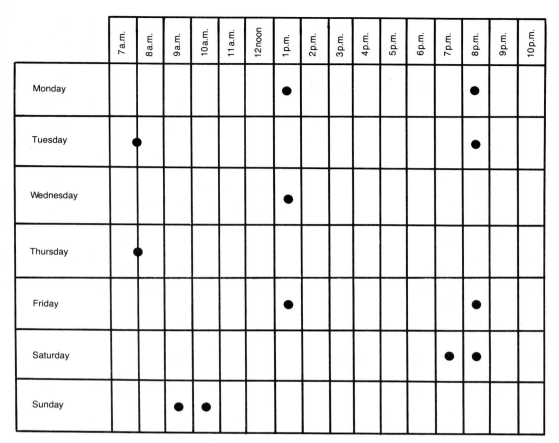

Fig 11 Training programme table.

achieved. Start by deciding what time during the week can regularly be given to training by filling in a programme outline (Fig 11). It is surprising what time can be found if there is a real intention to train.

Having decided on an outline timetable, allocate at least 75 per cent of the total time to those areas of fitness where the test scores were 3 or less. If all were of equal standard then the priority for improvement is (1) mobility, (2) posture, (3) stamina and endurance and (4) power and strength.

Avoid placing a stamina/endurance session before power and strength training.

Progressive Overload

Fitness is improved by working at a level that places the systems under a controlled stress. This causes a subsequent adaptation and increases the capacity for work.

Those with a low level of fitness when they start their training programme need not be concerned with how an overload may be achieved. Any training will lead to an improvement. Their immediate concern should be to ensure that they do not over-train and as a result cause injury. Fig 12 shows how monitoring condition during and after training can reduce the possibility of injury and undue stress.

	Slight fatigue (light load)	Marked fatigue (sub-maximum)	Extreme fatigue (maximum load)	Post-training symptons of overload
Complexion	Slight reddening	Marked reddening	Extreme reddening of pallor	Pallor remains over a number of days
Perspiration	Slight to medium	Heavy above waistline	Heavy over whole body	Perspiration at night
Execution of movement	Confident control	Frequent mistakes; uncertain control	Disturbance of co-ordination; loss of precision; staggering	Loss of co-ordination lasts 24–48 hours
Concentration	Normal no nervousness complete attention	Lack of attention reduced receptiveness	Loss of concentration reaction time longer	Loss of concentration lasts 24–48 hours
General health	No complaints	Muscular weakness	Tired muscles; pain in joints	Difficulty sleeping; pain in muscles and joints

Fig 12 The effects of training.

Progressive overload may be achieved in one or more of the following ways.

Increased Frequency

Increase the number of training sessions.

Increased Duration

Increase the length of a training session so that more work may be undertaken.

Increased Density

Increase the amount of work that is included in a training session by reducing the periods of rest and recovery.

Increased Intensity

Increase the speed or weight used. This method of increased overload is generally the last employed because it imposes the greatest stress.

Training Diaries

Once the initial enthusiasm that is usually associated with fitness has diminished, trainees frequently need rather more than the prospect of improved fitness to keep them highly motivated. Regular testing has already been mentioned as one method. Keeping a training diary is also helpful. Fig 13 shows an example of a recreational skier's diary. Note that a stamina points system is incorporated.

Fitness Training Record

Name: FRAN JONES   Month DEC. 1987

29 Nov		26 DEC		13 DEC		20 DEC		27 DEC	
MOBILITY (30min)		Mobility (30min)		Mobility				Mobility (30)	
Ex.Cycle (45min)	6½	Ex.Cycle (45min)	6½	Ex.Cycle (30)	3			Badminton (60)	4
						Posture (45m)		Posture (30)	
		Mobility (30m)				Mobility (30m)			
Posture (20min)		Posture (20m)		Posture (20m)				Ex.Cycle (45)	6½
Mobility (30m)				Mobility (30)		Ex.Cycle (60)	6		
Ex.Cycle (45m)	6½			Running (1hr)	20	Ex.Cycle (60)	6		
Mobility (30m)		Mobility (30m)							
		Ex.Cycle (30)	3						
Swimming (1hr)	10	Posture (30m)		Wt.Training					
		Running (30)	14	Ex.Cycle (30)	3	Wt.Training Mobility		Running (30)	14
Orienteering		Wt.Training							
Skiing (2hrs)	2	Skiing	2			Skiing (2hrs)	2		
	25		25½		26		14		24½

Fig 13 A training diary.

AGE-DEPENDENT TRAINING

One of skiing's great merits is that it is a family sport. It can be enjoyed by everyone irrespective of their age. Where adults and children are all skiers there may well be a temptation to make fitness training a family activity. This is inadvisable, particularly with the young. They are unable to tolerate the stressors imposed by an adult-orientated training programme and it can cause injuries, some of which may have a lasting detrimental effect. It is, for example, poss- ible to overtrain and strengthen muscles so much that the still-pliable long bones are distorted. There is also some suggestion that the high levels of lactic acid resulting from stamina training can have adverse effects.

It is not possible to give the exact age at which it is safe and therefore desirable for training to start. Each child's anatomical and physiological age differs from his or her actual age. Growth does not occur in all children at the same rate. It decreases from 25 cm in the first year to approximately 5 cm a year prior to the pubertal growth spurt. This occurs around the age of 12 in girls and 14 in boys. It marks the change from child- hood to adolescence and the start of grow- ing an adult body. As it may occur either early or late in both boys and girls, it is possible for maturational age to vary from 10 to 15 in children of 12 and 13 years of age.

Despite the difficulty, it is not unreason- able for parents to expect some guidance. While it is not possible to be precise, the training continuum (Fig 14) shows a system that can be adapted to meet all needs and abilities.

The intensity of training, indicated by the

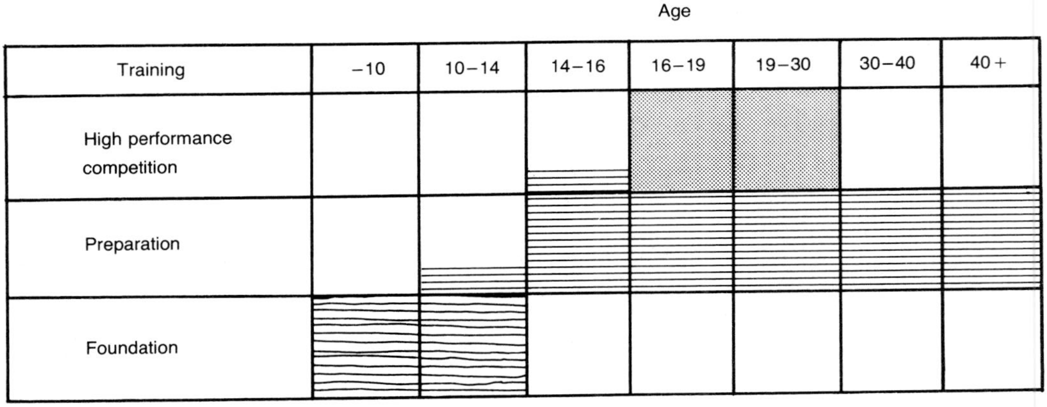

Age

Training	−10	10−14	14−16	16−19	19−30	30−40	40 +
High performance competition							
Preparation							
Foundation							

Fig 14 The training continuum.

closeness of the lines, increases with age and reaches peak levels after the age of 16 when the body is nearing adult proportions.

There is a gradual transition from one category of training to the next. The change from foundation training to preparation training might, for example, span a 4–6-month period.

All recreational skiers are included in the preparation training category. The high performance competition category is intended only for those who have aspirations to become competitors of national and international standard.

FOUNDATION TRAINING

Foundation training, as the name suggests, is the base on which all future development is dependent. It is not orientated to the needs of any one sport and a narrow discipline of technique but to the needs of each individual child. It should encourage the development of such qualities as balance, confidence, co-ordination and kinaesthesis. Skiing may be part of the process but should not be seen as being more important than any other games and activities. Children who specialise too young frequently do not live up to their parents' and trainers' expectations of them as teenagers and adults. Indeed the opposite is true: the best specialists are more often than not those whose foundation includes a great breadth and variety of activities. Versatility is the key to successful foundation training.

Traditional fitness training has no place in this stage of a child's development. However, mobility declines from about 8 years of age. It is sensible to encourage children to stay supple. This can be achieved by allowing them to do the exercises in Chapter 3.

While the emphasis is on physical preparation, the title Skiing Fit allows sufficient latitude to mention also foundation ski technique. It too is age dependent. Young children have a distinct style of their own. Their straight-legged, sitting-back style is caused by their centre of gravity being higher than that of an adult or teenager. It must be considered correct. No amount of telling will enable them to change until their bodies develop more adult proportions.

Just as inappropriate fitness training can cause injury to the young, so skiing can have a detrimental effect. If they wear ski boots that restrict normal ankle movement it places undue strain on the knee joint. Similarly,

Fig 15 The distinctive posture of a young child.

too much slalom pole training can cause tissue damage to the knee joint.

PREPARATION TRAINING

After puberty, young adolescents' skiing can benefit from fitness training. It must, of course, still be appropriate to their age and should not be as demanding as an adult's programme. It should be developed in the following order so that there is an emphasis on safety:

(1) mobility of the joints and major muscle groups
(2) muscular endurance and stamina
(3) strength and power

One of the greatest problems with this age group will be to keep their interest. Certainly, planning a versatile and interesting programme is the key as children are soon likely to become bored unless they are faced with varying challenges. It is also essential to set them a series of targets for improvement that are well within their reach. Nothing causes disillusionment and loss of interest more quickly than a sense of failure.

The combination of a training diary and the stamina points system has proved to be very successful with children in their early teens. The same points may be allocated as recommended in Chapter 5 but the weekly points target should be reduced to not more than 25 for a 14-year-old, increasing to 30–40 per week by the time they are 16 or 17.

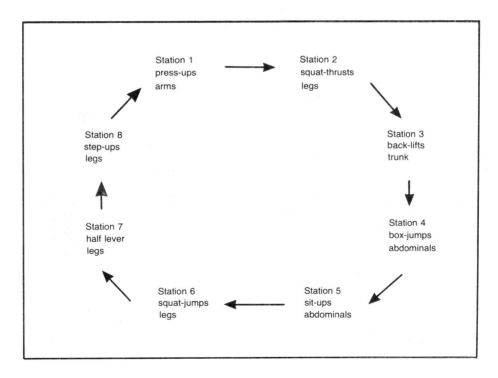

Fig 16 Circuit training layout.

Circuit Training

Circuit training is a very worthwhile activity for the younger age group. It is comparatively easy to organise and test. It does not need sophisticated equipment and because it uses only body-weight it is much safer than weight training for the young. Performers, depending on their level of fitness, complete one, two or three circuits of a series of exercises. The circuit is planned so that all the major muscle groups are included. When more than one exercise is included in the circuit for a particular muscle group they are alternated with other exercises.

The following exercises may be included in a circuit:

Stand on a bench or wooden block. Jump down to stand astride the bench, then return to the starting position. Keep the upper body and arms calm. (Fig 17.)

Stand to one side of a bench or cardboard box. Take off from two feet and jump across the bench to the other side. Return to the start. (Fig 18.)

Start in a front support position. Jump the feet in so that the knees touch the elbows. Return to the starting position. (Fig 19.)

Lie on the floor, legs straight and with the arms folded across the chest. Curl up and bend as far forwards as possible. Return to the starting position. (Fig 20.)

The degree of difficulty may be increased by bending the legs to a right angle and placing the feet flat on the floor. (Fig 21.)

Lie on the floor, hands behind the neck. Lift as far as possible. Return to the starting position. (Fig 22.)

Stand facing a chair or other object that is just below knee height. Step up on to the chair on the right foot. Close the left foot to the right. Step down on the right foot and return to the starting position. (Fig 23.)

Assume a front support position, hands at shoulder width. Lower the body in a straight line until the chest touches the floor. Return to the starting position again, keeping the body in a straight line. (Fig 24.)

Some find a good press-up difficult to do without allowing the trunk to bend. This is usually an indication of weak abdominal muscles. The exercises to improve posture (Chapter 4) help overcome this difficulty. Until a 'real' press-up is possible, the executive version exercises the shoulder girdle:

Kneel on the floor, support the trunk with hands at shoulder width. Lower the chest to the floor. Return to the starting position. (Fig 25.)

Fig 17 Astride jumps.

Fig 18 Box jumps.

Fig 19 Squat thrusts.

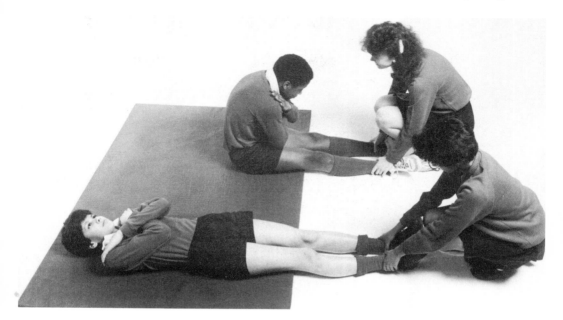

Fig 20 Sit-ups.

Fig 21 Modified sit-ups.

Fig 22 Back lifts.

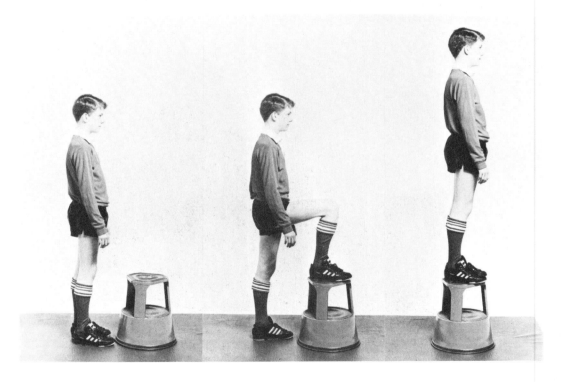

Fig 23 Step-ups.

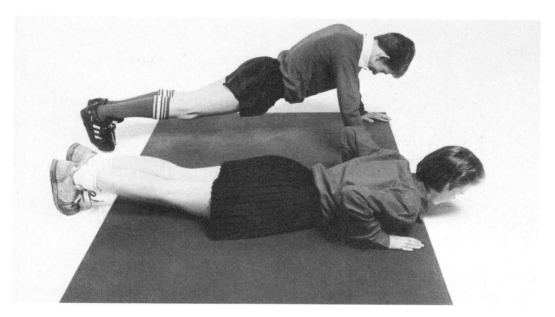

Fig 24 Press-ups.

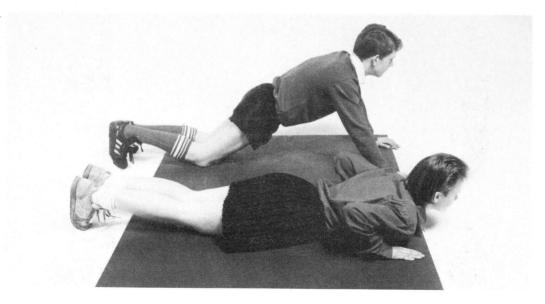

Fig 25 Executive press-ups.

Fig 26 Chin-ups.

All the previous exercises can be done without any special equipment. The following exercise requires a bar or beam placed at just above the stretch height:

Hang from the bar, palms of the hands facing backwards. Pull up until the chin is raised above the bar. Return to the starting position. (Fig 26.)

The number of repetitions of each exercise that should be included in every training session is determined by the following method.

Make a record card similar to that shown in Fig 27. This is used to record test scores and training loads. The exercises should be listed in the order that they will be performed.

First learn the correct techniques for each exercise. Then test to see how many repetitions of each exercise can be performed in one minute. It is preferable that the counting should be done by a partner and not by the person performing the tests. The reliability

Name: __ALISON WOODWARD__

Exercise	Date: 17:8:87		Date: 29:10:87		Date:	
	Test	Training	Test	Training	Test	Training
Sit-ups	36	18	42	21		
Squat-thrusts	65	33	68	34		
Back-lifts	70	35	72	36		
Press-ups	4	2	6	3		
Bench-jumps	80	40	86	43		
Leg-lifts	40	20	42	21		
Chins	1	1	2	1		
Step-ups	50	25	60	30		

Fig 27 A record card.

of the tests will also be increased if the pulse rate is allowed to return to its normal resting rate between each test.

The test result for each exercise is entered in the column headed 'Test'. This score is then halved and the number written in the next column. This is the number of repetitions that will be performed in each circuit. Every training session consists of one or more circuits where the training load for each exercise is completed without a break between exercises. A substantial recovery break is allowed between circuits.

Retesting should take place every 4–6 weeks and a new training load determined.

In addition to being very suitable for young adolescents, circuit training is recommended as being the most suitable exercise for adults who may be categorised as inactive. Certainly it will impose less stress on their system than weight training.

3 Mobility

Mobility is the freedom of movement of the joints and muscle groups.

Mobility must be given a high priority in any well-structured fitness training programme. Mobility of the lower back, the pelvic girdle, the thighs and the calves ensures that skiers assume the correct shapes and perform the techniques accurately. Muscle soreness and stiffness is a very common condition at the beginning of a skiing holiday. Both the incidence and the severity can be reduced by improving mobility prior to the holiday and by performing a few well-chosen exercises before and after each day's skiing. Improved mobility can limit the severity of an injury when the body is forced into very unnatural and painful shapes by the inevitable falls.

Mobility is improved by increasing the resting length of the muscles and ligaments. There are several methods for improving mobility. The most effective and safest is the *slow stretch method*.

Move the joint to the point where tightness and discomfort is felt in the muscles. Hold this position, relax the muscles and reduce the discomfort. Then move to a new limit of discomfort and hold the position for a further 10–15 seconds. Each exercise should be repeated three or four times at each training session.

The best results are achieved by stretching when the muscles are warm. Warm muscles can be obtained by a simple warm-up: five minutes walking or gentle jogging or using an exercise cycle. Others may prefer the easy option of doing their mobility exercises after a hot bath when the muscles are thoroughly warmed.

In the following illustrations all the demonstrators are shown performing the exercises wearing only T-shirts and shorts. This is to indicate the correct movements and body positions. Normally they would wear a tracksuit or weather suit so that body heat is retained and the exercises are more effective.

Sit on the floor in an upright position, legs straight and ankles together. Press the toes forwards and hold. Pull the toes back towards the knee, raising the heels from the floor and hold. (Fig 28.)

Stand about 1 metre away from a chair or a wall. Lean forwards and support your weight. Walk the feet backwards until the heels are raised from the floor. Keeping the hips pressed forwards, place the heels on the floor. (Fig 29.)

Crouch down and place the fingertips on the floor 10–15 cm in front of the toes. Straighten the legs as far as possible. When it is easy to straighten the legs with the fingertips on the floor, the degree of difficulty may be increased first by placing the hands flat on the floor and then by crossing the legs. (Figs 30–32.)

Kneel on the floor, knees and ankles together. Lean back and place the hands on the floor, fingers pointing backwards. The knees and ankles must be kept together in order to avoid placing undue strain on the knee joint. (Fig 33.)

Stand with the feet wide apart, hands on hips. Keeping the trunk upright and the seat tucked under, lower the hips to one side. Keep both feet flat on the floor. (Fig 34.)

Stand with the feet wide astride, front foot at right angles to the rear foot. Drop the hips towards the front foot keeping the rear foot flat on the floor. The head and trunk should be held upright and the seat tucked under. Repeat on the other side. (Fig 35.)

Sit on the floor with the heels drawn up to the seat. Hold the feet together and allow the weight of the legs to lower towards the floor. (Fig 36.)

Sit on the floor with one leg straight. The other leg is bent so that the sole of the foot rests against the inside of the thigh. Place a towel around the foot that is farthest away, use the towel to help pull the head towards the knee of the straight leg. Repeat on the other side. (Fig 37.)

Stand facing the back of a chair or obstacle at approximately hip height. Place the heel of one leg on the back of the chair. Keeping the supporting leg straight, fold forwards and place the head as near the raised knee as possible. (Fig 38.)

Stand feet astride, hands at the side. Slide one hand down the outside of the leg as far as possible without twisting the shoulders. Repeat to the other side. (Fig 39.)

Sit on the floor, legs straight and at right angles. Fold forwards and place the hands on the floor. If possible keep the toes and knees facing up. (Fig 40.)

Stand with the feet well apart, rear foot at right angles to the front foot. Slide the back foot along the floor as far as possible then straighten the front leg. Keep the body upright. (Fig 41.)

The following exercise, unlike the others, promotes mobility through active exercise:

Hold a hoop at waist height. Make the hoop swing around the waist by moving the hips in a circular motion. With improved efficiency place the hands on the head and try to keep the upper body and head as still as possible. (Fig 42.)

The importance of mobility cannot be over-emphasised. It must be given a very high priority in any well-structured training programme. Even those who score as high as 8 or 9 out of 10 in the two mobility tests should include at least two 25–30-minute sessions every week. Those who score less than 4 out of 10 should aim to complete at least five sessions per week until a more satisfactory standard is attained. As time is at a premium for many people, it may be necessary to exclude some facets of the programme until mobility has improved.

Mobility exercises should form the basis of warm-up and warm-down before and after other, more strenuous training.

If muscle soreness and stiffness is to be avoided or reduced in severity then a 15-minute mobility session should follow all skiing sessions.

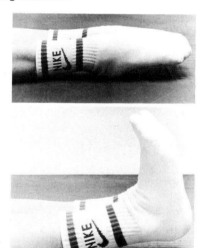

Fig 28 Ankle mobility.

Fig 29 Achilles, calf and hamstring stretch.

Fig 30 Moving from a crouching position to a straight leg.

Fig 31 Standing with a straight leg and hands on the floor.

Fig 32 Standing with crossed legs and hands on the floor.

Fig 33 Kneeling and leaning back.

Fig 34 The 'outrigger'.

Fig 35 The fencers' stretch (lunge).

Fig 36 The 'yoga' position.

Fig 37 Sitting hurdlers' stretch.

Fig 38 Standing hurdlers' stretch.

Fig 39 Side bends.

Fig 40 Straddle sit/reach.

Fig 41 Front splits.

Fig 42 The hula-hoop.

4 Posture

Posture is the shape of the body during performance of ski techniques and is a gauge of mechanical efficiency.

Of all the facets of fitness, posture has the greatest effect on a skier's technical ability. It is the determining factor in deciding whether a skier would be awarded 9 out of 10 for a near-perfect performance or 2 or 3 for something that is inaccurate and clumsy.

An almost uniform shape and movement pattern identifies the 'good' skiers and separates them from the 'not so good' who regrettably often think that they are doing the same thing.

A good posture or stance allows all skiers to learn the techniques of the sport correctly. A poor posture ensures that even the most basic techniques are learned and performed incorrectly. This invariably means that progress is slow and that real achievement is severely limited.

Analysis has shown that the major difference between those who ski with technical accuracy and those who do not is the shape of the pelvis and the lower back. The correct shape requires the front of the pelvis to be tilted upwards. The difference between this stance and an incorrect one is that the simple movement of the pelvis reduces the curvature of the lumbar spine, tucks the seat under and alters the angle of the femur or thighbone. It also rotates the femur outwards and causes a less knock-kneed stance and the ankle and knee to bend slightly. Only with this shape is it possible to turn the leg and point the skis into a new direction of travel without pushing the hip out and over-rotating it in the direction of the turn. The problem can be most easily identified in the performance of a snowplough turn. Those skiers who have a postural problem should first correct their snowplough technique; only if this is correct will the transition to more advanced turns be easy.

An incorrect skiing posture is often associated with a poor shape that is evident in normal everyday activity. Habitual bad posture increases with age as the muscles lose their tone.

When a different shape is required, as in skiing, the muscles are unable to either make the correct shape or retain it for a long period. The problem is compounded by the fact that many skiers are unable to identify the difference between the correct and incorrect shapes even when they can watch their movements in a mirror.

In order that an improvement in posture can be achieved, it is necessary to attend to both problems. Firstly, it is essential to be able to identify the correct and incorrect shape.

Stand sideways to a full-length mirror. Place both hands on the seat, allowing the stomach to protrude and the lower back to arch. Now contract the large muscles under the hands. The effect will be to change the angle of the pelvis, turn the knees outwards and cause the ankle and knee to bend slightly. Without losing the shape, move the hands and place them on the stomach muscles. Feel that they, too, have contracted and become firmer. (Fig 46.)

Turn to face the mirror. Repeat the first two stages of the above exercise. With the arms hanging loosely, keep the correct shape and step lightly from side to side. Try the same movements with a hollow back and the stomach protruding. It should feel awkward and clumsy – as it will when skiing. (Fig 47.)

Fig 43 Correct posture.

Fig 44 Incorrect posture.

41

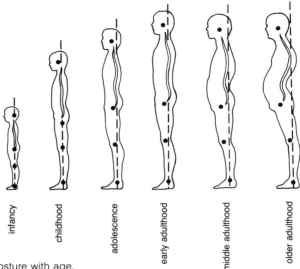

infancy

childhood

adolescence

early adulthood

middle adulthood

older adulthood

Fig 45 The change of posture with age.

Fig 46 Standing: lower back awareness.

Kneel on the floor with the knees hip-width apart, allowing the back to sag. Using the same muscles as in the previous exercises, flatten the back, pull the stomach up and tuck the seat under. (Fig 48.)

Repeat these exercises with and without a mirror until the correct and incorrect shapes are easily identified. Do not be in too much of a hurry to move on to the next section of exercises. Repetition of the above three will start to improve muscle tone, especially if the correct shape is held for 20 or 30 seconds.

In addition to the awareness exercises, try to improve posture in normal everyday activities. Do not allow the stomach to protrude and the back to sag. It gives the impression that there is excess weight around the middle when in fact it might just be poor posture!

Having improved shape awareness, the second stage is to strengthen the musculature that controls posture. Increased strength will cause the resting length of the muscles to be shortened, thereby allowing the

42

Fig 47 Side-stepping.

correct shape to be held more naturally and easily.

The pelvis is the largest and heaviest bone. Not surprisingly, then, it has a number of muscles acting on it and all must be strengthened in a well-structured training programme.

Sit on the floor, hands on knees and legs straight. Lean back as far as possible and hold as long as possible. Repeat 5–10 times (Fig 49.)

Take a front support (press-up) position, back flat and seat muscles tight. Resist a partner's attempts to 'break' the shape with pressure. Hold as long as possible. Repeat 5–10 times (Fig 50.)

Many find doing press-ups difficult. Usually the cause is a weakness in the muscles of the back and abdomen. Repetition of the preceding exercise will improve press-ups as well as posture.

Fig 48 Kneeling: lower back awareness.

Fig 49 Lean back as far as you can while gripping your knees.

Fig 50 Trunk resistance.

Lie on the floor, feet hip-width apart and legs bent. Lift the seat as high as possible and hold as long as possible. Repeat 5–10 times. The degree of difficulty may be increased by a partner trying to 'break' the shape by pressing on the pelvis. (Fig 51.)

Lie on the floor, legs straight and arms at the side. Press the small of the back onto the floor and hold as long as possible. Repeat 5–10 times. (Fig 52.)

Stand upright, if necessary supporting the weight on the back of a chair. Lift one leg sideways and hold as long as possible. Keep the trunk upright. Repeat 5–10 times. Repeat on the other leg. (Fig 53.)

Lie on the floor. Lift the top leg and hold as long as possible. Repeat 5–10 times. Repeat on the other side. Again the degree of difficulty may be increased by a training partner offering a resistance and trying to break the shape. Alternatively, the exercise may be performed wearing ski boots to increase the difficulty. (Fig 54.)

Lie face down on the floor, arms crossed under the head. Raise the feet and hold. Repeat 5–10 times. Partner resistance may also be used. (Fig 55.)

The third and perhaps most important phase in the improvement of posture is the application of the newly acquired awareness and strength to the techniques of skiing.

Choose a gentle slope on snow or an artificial facility where the gradient will not cause any apprehension or nervousness and where it is possible to concentrate only on the correct shape.

Stand at the top of the slope with the skis on a flat area or firmly across the fall-line. Repeat the movements experienced and learned in the first exercise in front of the mirror. Allow the lower back to become hollow and the stomach to sag forwards. Tighten the muscles that improve posture. Next turn and schuss down the slope in an open stance with the pelvis in the correct position. Do not attempt to turn. Repeat the exercise until the shape feels comfortable and familiar. Only when this has been

Fig 51 The bent hip lift.

Fig 52 Small of back press.

Fig 53 Standing: side leg lift.

Fig 54 Lying: side leg raise.

46

Fig 55 Prone leg lift.

learned move on to the next stage: continue to schuss but deliberately move the pelvis to a poor posture and then return to a correct posture. This will reinforce the learning process and increase awareness.

Learning to turn while retaining the correct shape is the next task. Many experienced skiers will be tempted by their egos to do this while trying intermediate or advanced turns on more difficult terrain. More often than not this will inhibit learning and real progress. It is preferable to stay on easy slopes where the concentration for the acquisition of new skills is not disrupted by other factors.

The snowplough is the first turn learned and arguably the most important. Anyone who is capable of doing a perfect snowplough is capable of learning more advanced techniques more easily than someone who cannot snowplough correctly. From the schuss move to a snowplough in the fall-line. Repeat the awareness exercises, moving from a correct to an incorrect shape. Then

move to wide-radius turns. Concentrate on steering the foot into the new direction of travel with the lower back rounded. Do not allow the hip on the outside of the turn to push sideways or to be overrotated in the direction of the turn. When this feels familiar try a few turns with a deliberately poor posture. It should feel awkward and uncomfortable. Learn to recognise the different feel between the correct and incorrect method. When and only when the correct shape is instinctive move on to more difficult turns.

Two groups are likely to experience more than average difficulty with their ski posture.

Those with a larger than average frame who are 'bulky' around the middle and hips often find both making and retaining the correct shape very difficult. A lack of mobility is usually the cause. The problem may therefore be minimised by improving mobility before attempting to improve posture.

The second and bigger group are women, who will find conforming to a male-orientated technical base extremely difficult. Their

47

Fig 56 Incorrect pelvic posture.

Fig 57 Incorrect arm carriage.

Fig 58 A natural (and correct) position for
the arms.

Fig 59 Another example of a good position for
the arms.

difficulty is caused by the different anatomical structure of their pelvis and femur. As a
consequence, it is extremely difficult for
them to turn the leg and steer the ski without
some lateral movement and rotation of the
hips. Nevertheless, improving the tone and
strength of the muscles will bring about
some improvement.

Another exclusively female problem is
caused by wearing high-heeled shoes. In
order to balance in high heels a realignment
of the spine, pelvis and legs is necessary. As
well as changing the position of the pelvis,
it can also cause a permanent shortening of
the Achilles tendon, resulting in a stiffness of
the ankle joint that makes the kneeling

action during a ski turn difficult. This problem may be reduced by increasing the
mobility of the ankle joint.

One final contributory factor to poor posture applies to men and women alike. It is
often exaggerated by an incorrect carriage
of the arms. Many skiers either hold their
arms too high or pull their elbows back.
This rotates the shoulders backwards, increases the curvature of the lumbar spine
and tilts the pelvis forward.

A more natural and correct arm position
is with the upper arm near-vertical from the
shoulder to the elbow and the elbow bent in
order that the hands are carried in front.

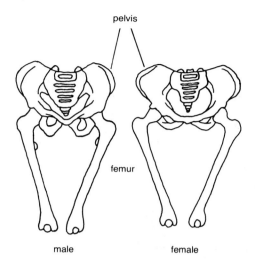

Fig 60 The male and female pelvis.

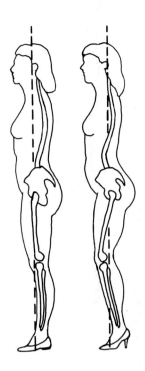

Fig 61 The effect of wearing high heels on posture.

5 Stamina and Muscular Endurance

Stamina and *muscular endurance* permit an individual to delay the onset of fatigue and to continue working.

These two facets of fitness are vitally important to recreational skiers. Without them the massive workload imposed by skiing, the effects of altitude and even limited après skiing, causes extreme fatigue. This is a contributory factor in many accidents, as analysis has shown that skilled performance breaks down as muscles become tired. Similarly, decision making can be adversely affected by fatigue. A lack of stamina and muscular endurance is responsible for skiers losing many hours of practice time as fatigue forces them to leave the pistes early.

Stamina is determined by the efficiency of the heart and lungs in transporting oxygen to the working organs and muscles and in removing the waste products of exercise.

Muscular endurance is dependent on the ability of the muscles to absorb and use the oxygen and to dispose of the waste.

Stamina training increases the number of red blood cells, which carry the oxygen to the tissues. The volume of blood that is pumped from the heart with each heartbeat is also increased. These two changes ensure that the resting pulse is lower and that the maximum rate during medium and heavy workloads is also decreased. The rate of breathing also reduces during periods of work.

Muscular endurance training increases the number of small blood vessels and as a consequence permits a more efficient exchange of the fuel, oxygen and waste products.

Improving both abilities reduces the recovery time following medium and heavy workloads. Skiers who take the trouble to improve both are therefore likely to be able to start each day's skiing in a better condition than those who do not.

Both abilities are improved by undertaking exercise that causes a sustained increase in the heart rate. The type of exercise is not critical to obtain an improvement in stamina. But an improvement in the endurance of the leg muscles will be obtained only by working the legs.

Training is most beneficial if each session lasts at least 25 minutes and follows the pattern shown in Fig 62.

Following a short warm-up – a few stretching exercises will suffice – the training session is started. The pulse rate is increased and is maintained at a steady rate. Ideally the pulse rate should be monitored with an accurate pulse metre so that each individual can work at the correct level for his or her age. This is determined using the following formula. The trainee's age is deducted from 220 and the optimum training rate is between 70 and 85 per cent of that figure. For a 35-year-old, for example:

$$\begin{array}{r} 220 \\ -35 \quad \text{(trainee's age)} \\ \hline 185 \end{array}$$

Training rate: 130–58 beats per minute.

Fig 63 shows the optimum training rates for all age groups. Note that there is a steady decrease with age.

The amount of training that each individual should undertake is dependent on

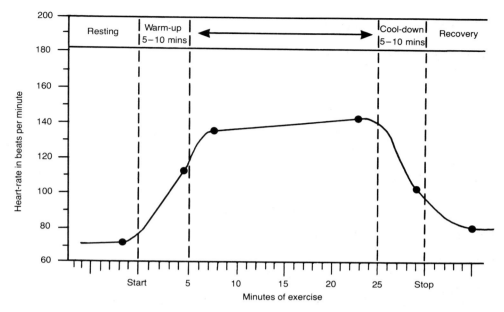

Fig 62 Training heart beat pattern.

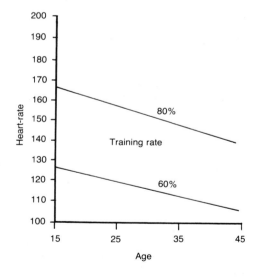

Fig 63 Optimum age-related heart rate when training.

their age, their standard of fitness and, of course, the time that is available each week. The system shown in Fig 64 allows every-one to accumulate a weekly points target by participating in their preferred or most easily available activities. Points are allocated to each activity according to the severity of the exercises. A weighting has also been given to those activities that develop stamina and the endurance of the leg muscles.

Of the activities listed, running and jogging score the highest. However, everyone should not feel compelled to gain some of their points in this way. For many even the thought of running any distance is a daunting prospect and the activity itself a severe punishment. Those people will simply have to find other ways of accumulating their points.

It is, of course, a matter of personal preference but for those who require some guidance, cycling has much to commend it to the needs of skiers. The pedalling action is similar to the independent leg action of proficient skiers. Also, providing that the

53

Activity	Points
Running/jogging	4 points per mile
Walking (urban)	1 point per mile
Walking (hill/mountain)	2 points per mile + 3 points for each 1000 ft of ascent
Cycling (road)	2 points per mile
Cycling (machine)	1 point per 10 minutes
Skipping	2 points per 10 minutes
Skiing (artificial slope)	1 point per 10 minutes continuous activity. NB No use of lifts permitted!
Squash	1 point per game
Badminton	1 point per game
Tennis	1 point per set
Hockey	3 points per game
Football	3 points per game
Football (5-a-side)	1 point per 10 minutes
Swimming: butterfly	2 points per 100 metres
crawl/backstroke	1 point per 100 metres
breaststroke	1 point per 100 metres

Fig 64   Points allocation for selected activities.

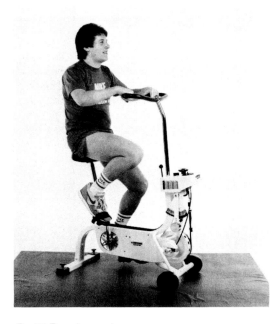

Fig 65 Exercise cycle.

weight is supported on the ball of the foot and that the leg is fully straightened, it uses the same muscles as skiing, including some that affect posture. For those for whom cycling on the road has no appeal either, an exercise bike is a viable alternative. The obvious advantage is that users do not have to contend with congested and dangerous traffic. In addition, a good exercise cycle has a 'built-in' timer so that the duration of exercise can be timed accurately. The resistance can be varied so that the machine may be used with equal effect for strength and power training in addition to stamina and endurance. Also it is much easier to measure and vary the pulse rate within the optimum training range than it is with any other form of exercise. Some users have even found that this form of exercise can be combined most easily with reading or listening to a personal stereo!

Skiing on an artificial facility has been included in the training programme.

However, it must be pointed out that strict limitations have been stipulated in order to obtain a suitable workload. Analysis has shown that under normal conditions of use it is most unlikely that the workload is sufficient to have any worthwhile effect on fitness. Preparatory fitness is as necessary for learning to ski on an artificial facility as it is on snow.

Having selected the preferred activities it is then necessary to set a weekly points target for the start of the training programme. This should be determined by each individual's current level of fitness as measured in the 12-minute test and his or her age. Fig 66 gives suggested targets that will ensure adequate initial workloads but will also prevent those who are comparatively unfit from suffering undue stress.

Once the training programme has been established, it will be necessary to increase gradually the weekly total in order to create

	Age			
Test	Under 20	20–30	30–40	Over 40
5	30+	30	20–30	20
4	30+	25–30	20–25	15–20
3	25+	20–25	15–20	15
2	20+	15–20	10–15	10
1	15–20	15	10–15	10
0	10	10	10	5–10

Fig 66 Initial points targets.

an overload and obtain a further improvement in the level of fitness. A reasonable long-term goal is to increase the initial score by 50–75 per cent over a 4–6-month period, adding not more than 5 points per week after the first six weeks of the training programme.

6 Strength and Power

Just as fitness and health are often mistakenly portrayed as being the same, so too are strength and power frequently confused. In fact each has distinct characteristics and a different application to ski technique.

STRENGTH

Strength is the ability to exert a force against a resistance. Its importance to recreational skiers is that it enables them to avoid serious injury when they fall and when the legs are subjected to great stress as the skis stop and the body is rotated over the top of the skis. Only if the skier is strong enough to keep the legs rigid can the possibility of injury be reduced.

Strength also determines one's ability to hold the leg in the correct position during ski turns. There is a direct relationship between the speed of the turn and the strength requirement. The higher the speed the greater the force and the greater the strength that must be used to hold the shape. Downhillers, and those who aspire to match their speed, require the greatest strength as they are subjected to immense forces during their long-radius turns. They must also demonstrate the same strength when they fall by keeping their legs straight if at all possible.

Strength is usually measured by determining the maximum load that can be lifted in one lift. The heavier the load that can be lifted, the stronger the muscles.

WEIGHT TRAINING

Weight training, at one time considered unsuitable for many sports because it was thought to inhibit speed, has, with an increase in knowledge, been accepted as an essential part of fitness training. The increased availability of all forms of weight training equipment in both municipal and private facilities should ensure that more people will be able to use this form of training. Participation must, however, be subject to very strict rules to ensure the safety of the participants. The age at which it is introduced must be controlled as chronic injury can result. Prepubescent trainees should not be permitted to use weights, and young adolescents should use only light weights. The techniques must be learned correctly. It follows, therefore, that trainees of all ages must be taught by qualified, knowledgeable coaches who will be able to determine the correct training schedules for each individual.

The dilemma faced by coaches is not whether to introduce weight training but which system to utilise – traditional weights or the new machines. The machine-based programmes are considered to be safer than the traditional method: 'safety factors are inherent in the design of each station which accommodates a wide range of physiques and capacities'. Over a lengthy period no accidents or injuries were found with extensive use of the machine. Organisational problems are fewer with machine-based programmes as it is comparatively easy to change the weights. Given the luxury of a choice, it would seem the machines have an obvious advantage over the traditional method.

One of the most important considerations is when to introduce weight training into a young athlete's programme. There is no absolute rule. The decision must be based on maturational readiness to change to a training regime that imposes more stress on the individual. It is wise to wait until the pubertal growth spurt has terminated and the bones, ligaments and muscular attachments are less likely to be injured. Test scores attained in circuit training may be used as an indication of a readiness to start weight training. An individual who is able to achieve the scores in Fig 67 is unlikely to suffer any adverse effects from weight training.

	Girls	Boys
Press-ups	35	45
Sit-ups	40	50
Squat thrusts	50	55
Pull-ups	15	20
Leg lifts	40	45
Bench jumps	70	80

Fig 67

Training Methods

The training method employed is entirely dependent on the performer's fitness levels and the training objectives. To ensure safety and reduce the possibility of stress injuries, the hierarchical structure discussed in the principles of training is applied to weight training and the following are developed in order: (1) mobility of the joints, (2) stamina, (3) local muscular endurance, (4) strength and power through the range of movement.

When stamina and local muscular endurance are the objectives, the weight is low and the number of repetitions is high. When strength is the objective, the weight is high and the number of repetitions is low. When power is the objective, the number of repetitions in a given time is high and the weight is again comparatively low.

Training Load Determination

It is absolutely essential to quantify each individual's training load accurately if the training is to have the desired effect and if the possibility of training injury is to be reduced to a minimum. The following system is recommended.

(1) Test the maximum weight that can be lifted in one lift as the training load must always be determined as a percentage of the maximum. To avoid injury work up to the maximum.

(2) Categorise the training load according to the objective of the training. Low load: 35–50 per cent maximum; medium load: 55–60 per cent maximum; high load: 70–100 per cent maximum. This system applies where endurance or strength are the objectives. It is necessary to utilise another system of training load determination when power or power-endurance is the objective. Since speed of movement is the requirement of the vast majority of ski techniques, it is necessary to adopt a training programme that will improve this aspect of fitness. Research by Moffroid and Whipple has established that 'High power [high speed, low load] exercises produced increases in muscular force at all speeds of contraction at and below the training speed' and 'High power exercises increase muscular endurance at high speeds more than low power [low speed, high load] exercises endurance at low speeds'.

(a) Test the maximum possible.
(b) Set a low load (35–50 per cent maximum). Test the maximum repetitions that can be performed in a given time, usually one minute.
(c) Determine the training programme to create an overload: 2 sets × 60 per cent of

Exercise	Weight (max.)	Weight	Weight	Weight
	Reps	Reps	Reps	Reps
Abdominals	160	80		
		3×8		
Leg extension	110	60		
		3×8		
Pull-over	130	70		
		3×8		
Leg curls	80	40		
		3×8		
Rotary torso	70	40		
		3×8		
Abductors	80	40		
		3×8		
Adductors	90	50		
		3×8		
Double chest	110	60		
		3×8		
Lower back	180	90		
		3×8		
Duo squat	260	140		
		3×8		
Double shoulder	110	60		
		3×8		

Fig 68 The multiple set system.

repetitions maximum, 3 sets × 45 per cent repetitions maximum.

Retest every 6–8 weeks and change training programme according to test results and current objectives.

There are several different methods of working with weights. Each method is designed to help achieve specific objectives and is suited to the needs of the individual.

Exercise	Weight (max.) Reps	Weight Reps	Weight Reps	Weight Reps
Abdominals	80	50	50	
		1×8	1×10	
Leg extension	90	50	50	
		1×8	1×10	
Pull-over	140	70	70	
		1×8	1×10	
Leg curls	50	30	30	
		1×8	1×10	
Rotary torso	70	40	40	
		1×8	1×10	
Abductors	70	40	40	
		1×8	1×10	
Adductors	70	40	40	
		1×8	1×10	
Double chest	60	40	40	
		1×8	1×10	
Lower back	90	50	50	
		1×8	1×10	
Duo squat	160	90	90	
		1×8	1×10	
Double shoulder	40	20	20	
		1×8	1×10	

Fig 69 The multiple set system.

Single Set

This consists of performing one set using one muscle group followed by another set using a different muscle group in the same manner as circuit training. The performers complete all the exercises in the circuit once. Additional loading is achieved by increasing the number of repetitions in a set or by completing more than one circuit. It is a method suitable for use by those starting weight training.

Multiple Set System

Multiple sets may be classified as interval training. Performers complete 2–8 sets with a recovery break between sets before moving to a new exercise. This system is suited to power endurance training.

Multiple Set System: Flushing

This variation of the multiple set system requires the performer to complete a number of sets of different exercises all working the same muscle group. The system has the effect of greatly increasing the blood flow in the muscle group in use. This is termed 'flushing' and increases local endurance.

Multiple Set System: Pyramids

This system derives its name from the pattern of progression of the exercises. Starting from a broad base of five or six repetitions in a set with a comparatively low weight, the number of repetitions is gradually reduced as the load is increased. The last set contains only one repetition with a maximum or near-maximum load. The recovery break indicative of interval training is taken between sets. It is a system designed for maximum strength development.

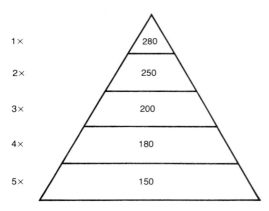

Fig 70 The multiple set system (pyramids).

The following illustrate the exercises that may be performed on a Powersport Multi-gym, one of the most popular weight training machines. Both the diagrams and description of the exercises are of immense benefit to both trainees and coaches.

Supine Bench Press

This exercises the chest, front of the shoulder and rear of the upper arm.

Lie flat on bench, head towards the machine and feet shoulder-width apart on the floor. Take overgrasp grip on handlebar with the elbows turned out, hands directly above elbows. The handlebar should be directly above the sternum (breastbone). Take a breath before commencing effort. Press handlebar upwards and lock out elbows. Exhale on completion of lift. Keep your back flat on the bench at all times. Lower the handlebar to the start position under control and repeat.

Side Lateral Bends

This exercises the side of the trunk.

Stand sideways on to the machine with the outside of the thigh almost touching the handgrip and let the arm hang straight. Bend sideways until you can grip handle. Keeping the elbow straight and the arm close to the body, lift the bar by bending sideways away from the machine as far as possible. Hold for two seconds, return slowly to start position and repeat.

Seated Leg Press

This is a good general exercise for the whole of the legs.

Sit on the seat with your feet on the floor. Adjust the seat along the sliding rail so your knees are about 10 cm clear of the footplate. (This ensures your knees are not too deeply bent when you place your feet on the footpads.) Place both feet firmly on the footpads

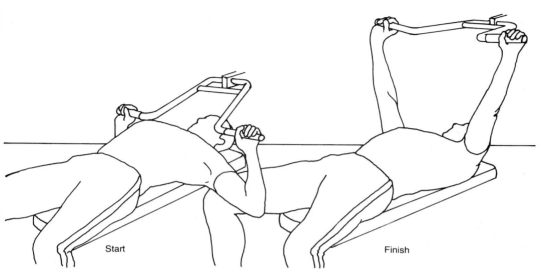

Start

Finish

Fig 71 Supine bench press.

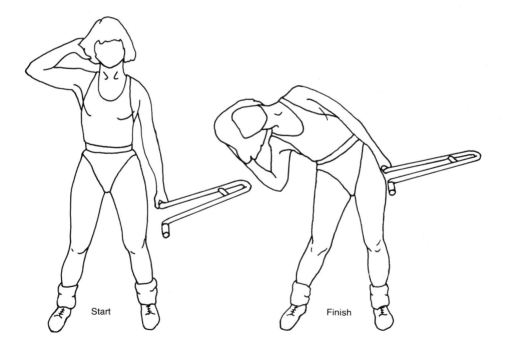

Start

Finish

Fig 72 Side lateral bend.

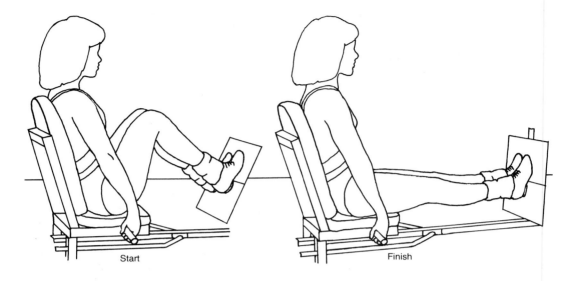

Start   Finish

Fig 73 Seated leg press.

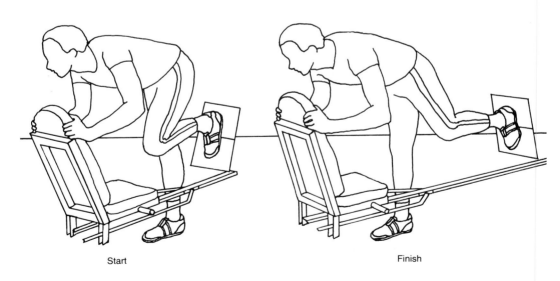

Start   Finish

Fig 74 Sprinter's leg drive.

with no part of the foot outside the footpad area. Grip the handgrips and, keeping your back firmly against the backrest, push your feet away smoothly and under control until your knees are locked out. Return slowly and repeat. Breathe out as you press – in on return.

Sprinters Leg Drive

This exercise develops the hip extensor muscles used in sprinting.

Face away from the machine with one foot placed centrally on the footpad and the other on the floor approximately midway along the chrome seated rail. Hold the rear of the seat and adopt a semi-crouch position with a flat back. Push your leg backwards but always under control – do not allow the footplate to accelerate too fast. Emphasise the last 15° of lock-out in the leg to streng-then both the knee and hip extensors.

Return the weight under control and repeat. This is a unilateral exercise (one leg) and so both must be repeated separately.

Lat Pull-Down

This exercises the large back muscles, plus the chest and front of the upper arms.

(1) *Behind Neck* Kneel facing the machine so that the lat bar is directly above the tip of the shoulders. Keep the back straight and with arms fully extended grasp the bar in a wide overgrasp grip. Pull the bar down until it touches the back of the neck, also ensuring that the elbows have been drawn down to the sides of the body and slightly backwards. Tilt the head forward during the pull, exhale on pull, inhale on return stroke.

(2) *To Chest* Position as above, except kneel further away from the machine so that the bar is approximately 30 cm in front of the line of the shoulders. Pull down to chest.

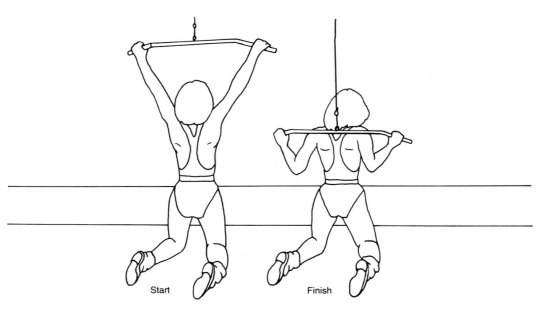

Start   Finish

Fig 75 Latissimus pull-down.

Tricep Push-Down

This exercise isolates the muscles at the back of the arm.

Stand facing the machine, holding the bar with a narrow grip. Lock the elbows to the side of the trunk so that only the elbow (not the shoulders) is used in the movement. Push down and extend the forearms fully until the elbows are locked out. Hold for about one second and push down with hands. Return to the starting position under control and repeat. Exhale on downward stroke, inhale on return.

Seated Pulley Rowing

This exercises the upper back, rear of the shoulders and front of the upper arm.

Sit facing the weight stack. Place your feet on the footpads, knees straight or slightly flexed. Take overgrasp grip on the bar. Keeping the body straight with a flat back, pull the bar into the chest. To produce the maximum benefit for the upper back, keep the elbow high in line with the shoulders and pull the hands to the front of the shoulders.

To work the lower back (latissimus dorsi) and the back of the shoulders, reverse the grip to undergrasp and pull the bar into the midriff, keeping the elbows tucked in at your side. Return to starting position under control and do not allow the weights to snap the body forward at the start or end of each repetition. Breathe in as you pull, breathe out on the return stroke.

Bicep Curl (Arm Curl)

This exercises the front of the upper arm and forearm.

This exercise may be performed in a standing or kneeling position. In either case it is necessary to have a wide base, feet or knees apart to give stability to the trunk. Also stand or kneel as close to the footpads as possible so that the pull on the cable is

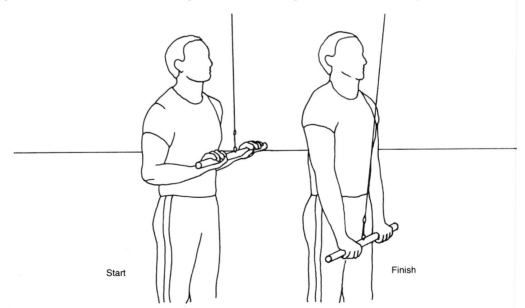

Start   Finish

Fig 76 Tricep push-down.

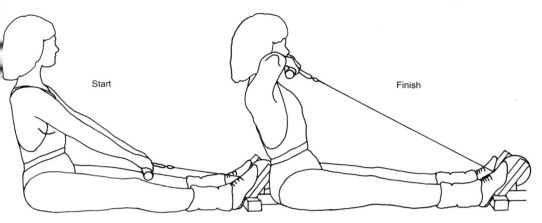

Fig 77 Seated pulley rowing.

near-vertical. Hold the handlebar under-grasp about shoulder-width apart with arms hanging straight down at your side. Keeping the upper arm still and elbows tucked in by your sides curl the bar up to your chest by bending the elbows, hold the bar at full contraction for a second, lower and repeat. Breathe in as you lift the weight, breathe out on the return. Do not rock the hips during the movement. As a variation, use a single arm with stirrup handle, perhaps twisting the hand at the top of the stroke.

Bent-Over Rowing

This exercises the back, rear of the shoulder and front of the upper arm.

Stand facing the machine with the feet approximately shoulder-width apart and toes turning outwards slightly. Bend the knees (unlock them) to reduce strain on lower back and hamstrings and keep the back flat with your bottom sticking out. Keep your head up. Grasp the bar (palms down) about shoulder-width apart and pull the bar strongly to the chest or abdomen by flexing the elbows and pulling them backwards and upwards. If the bar is pulled to a high chest position, the exercise will affect the upper back and shoulder muscles; if to the abdomen, the middle and lower part of the latissimus dorsi. Lower the bar under control. Breathe in on pull, out on return.

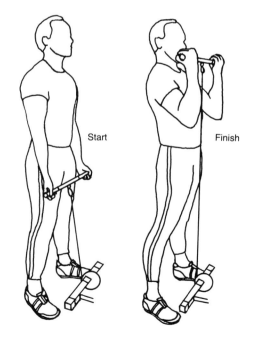

Fig 78 Bicep curl (arm curl).

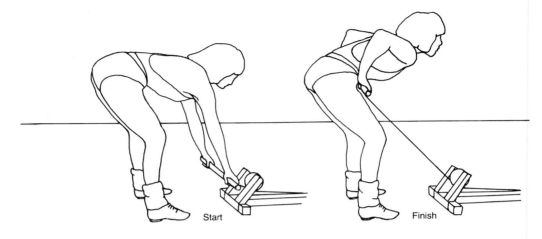

Fig 79 Bent-over rowing.

Bent-Leg Dead Lift

This exercises the lower back, buttocks and thighs.

Stand astride the foot pads, facing the machine and with feet about hip-width apart. Grasp the bar in an overgrasp grip. Get into the starting position by bending at the knees, keeping the back flat with your bottom pushed out, as if sitting onto a chair. Keep your head up, looking forward. Lift using your legs only. Arms are straight, knees are fully locked out. Return to starting position by bending at the knees and repeat. Exhale as you lift, breathe in on return stroke.

NB This exercise is not recommended for users who suffer from back pain.

Seated Shoulder Press

This exercises the shoulders and rear of the upper arm.

Sit on the stool facing towards the machine. Position the stool so that the handles are in line with the front of the chest and at shoulder height. Keep your back straight

and feet planted firmly on the footrests, hands slightly wider than shoulder-width apart. Lock the wrists. Breathe in and exhale sharply as you push the bar up. Lean the

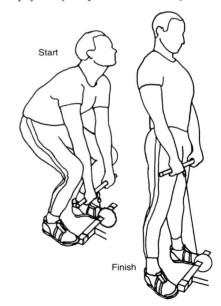

Fig 80 Bent-leg dead lift.

trunk slightly forward (but keeping a straight back) as you complete the lift. Lower under control and repeat.

Press Behind Neck

This exercises the shoulders and rear of the upper arm.

Sit on the stool facing away from the machine. In the starting position the bar should be roughly in line with the front of the shoulder. Keep your back flat and feet firmly on the footrests or the floor. Hand position as in seated shoulder press. Push up but avoid the tendency to lean back towards the machine. Breathe in and exhale sharply as you push the bar up.

Leg Extension

This is an exercise for the front of the thigh (quadriceps) or knee extensors.

Sit on the machine with your neck straight and the knee joint in line with the pivot of the lever arm. Hold the sides of the frame with your hands and lock your feet behind the padded rollers. The roller should be resting on the front of the lower leg. Extend both legs until the knees are fully locked out and pull your toes back towards the knees on lock-out. Hold briefly, then return under control to the start position and repeat. Breathe out as you push up and in on the return.

Leg Curls

This is an exercise for the rear of the thighs (hamstrings).

Lie flat down on the bench with your head towards the machine. Your knees should extend over the end of the bench so the

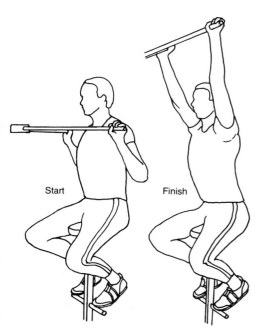

Start   Finish

Fig 81 Seated shoulder press.

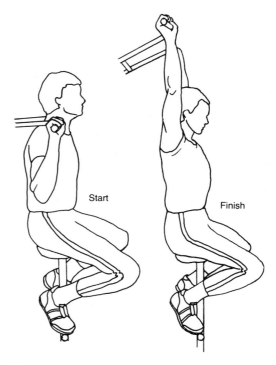

Start   Finish

Fig 82 Press behind neck.

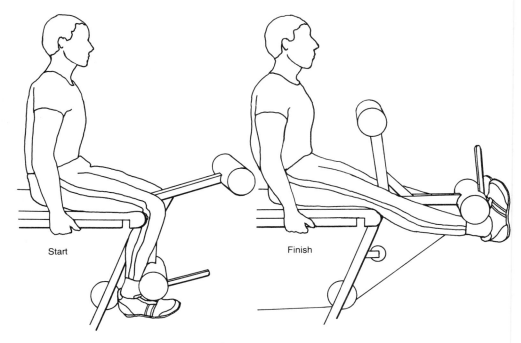

Start

Finish

Fig 83 Leg extension.

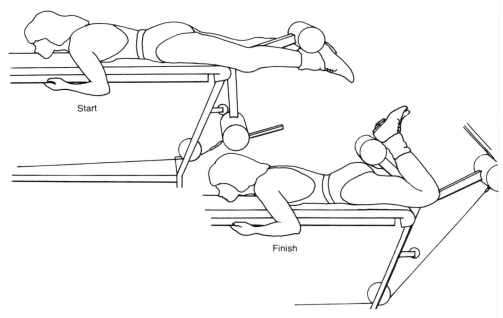

Start

Finish

Fig 84 Leg curl.

knee joint is in line with the pivot of the lever arm. Place the heels under the padded roller. Grip the bench with your hands and curl the lower leg until the knee is at right angles to the upper thigh. Hold and return to the starting position and repeat. Breathe on every repetition.

Upright Rowing

This is an excellent shoulder exercise which also works the shoulder blades (scapulae) and elbow flexors (biceps).

Stand with the feet slightly more than shoulder-width apart, straddling the footpads. Hold the bar overgrasp (palms down, hands about 15 cm apart. Breathe in as you pull the bar up to the chin, keeping the elbows flared out and above the line of the bar at all times. The elbows should also be fully flexed at the top of the pull. Lower the bar slowly and repeat, exhaling as you do so.

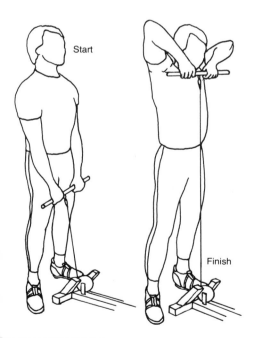

Fig 85 Upright rowing.

Straight-Arm Pullover

This is an excellent development exercise for the chest and back.

Lie on your back, head towards the machine, with your arms extended directly above your head. Hold the bar, overgrasp grip, and pull the bar over your head and down to your hips. Remember to turn your head to one side to keep it clear of the cable. You may also need to brace your feet under a bench to avoid slipping backwards towards the machine. Keep your back as flat as possible against the floor through the whole exercise. Return to the starting position under control. Breathe in prior to commencing but thereafter breathe out during the pull once the bar has passed vertically overhead, and breathe in on return once the bar has again passed the vertical position on the return stroke.

Bent-Knee Sit-Ups

This is an exercise to tone up the stomach and the trunk.

If exercising for the first time, place the abdominal board on its lowest setting or flat on the floor. As you become stronger the board can be raised higher on the ladder. Lie on the board with your insteps tucked under the foot rollers and knees bent. Place your hands loosely by the side of your head but do not interlock the fingers. *Interlacing the fingers allows you to pull the head forward with possible risk of neck injury.* Sit up until your elbows touch your knees, concentrating on curling the trunk forward and tucking your chin on to your chest. Hold, return under control and repeat. Breathe out as you sit up, breathe in on the return.

Leg Raise

This is an exercise for the lower abdominal area.

Place the abdominal board in its lowest

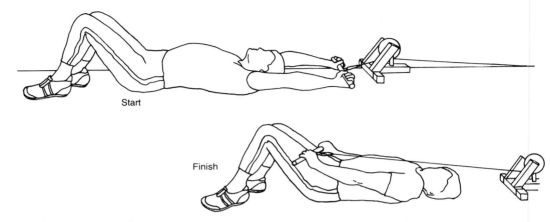

Fig 86 Straight-arm pullover.

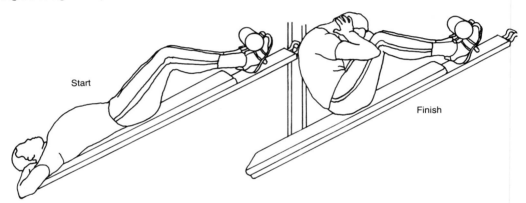

Fig 87 Bent-knee sit-up.

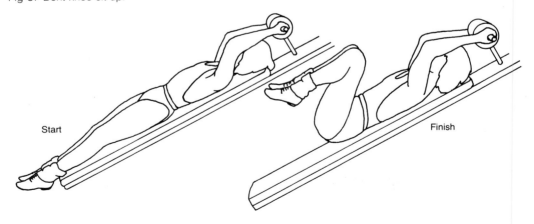

Fig 88 Leg raise.

position and lie flat on your back (supine) with your head towards the padded rollers. Grasp the hand-grips, breathe in and pull your knees up to your chest. Hold, then lower down slowly whilst breathing out and repeat. To make the exercise harder incline the board more.

Back Hyperextension

This exercise strengthens the back and tones up the buttocks.

Adjust the pads so that they rest on the top of your thighs and support the pelvis when in the start position, with your knees straight. Place your heels firmly under the footrest and make sure the soles of your feet are firmly against the back rail. Keep your legs straight and the pads supporting the thighs. Lower your trunk into the start position. Place your hands on the back of the thighs if you are a beginner, and as you get stronger move them to a position behind your head. Raise your trunk smoothly upwards under control until the trunk and legs are in a straight line with head up and looking forward. *Do not* overextend as this may lead to compression of the vertebrae, with possible back injury, and *do not* throw your head back too far. Hold the finish

position for two seconds then lower gently under control. Breathe out as you raise up and in on the return.

Extended Sit-Up

This is an advanced exercise for the trunk.

Sit facing the machine with the pads directly under your buttocks, legs straight with your feet tucked under the foot roller. Place your hands loosely by the sides of your head and allow yourself to sit back slowly and under control. Do not go much beyond horizontal, then pull your trunk back up to the start position. Pause and repeat – again in a slow and controlled manner. Breathe in as you sit back, out as you pull up. Breathe on every repetition.

For those who do not wish or who are unable to lose weight, the following exercises will also lead to an improvement of strength. They do have the advantage that they can be done without having to travel to a specialist facility.

The single leg lifts used in the fitness tests may be used. The workload may be increased by placing some sand in a plastic bag and then placing this in a rucksack

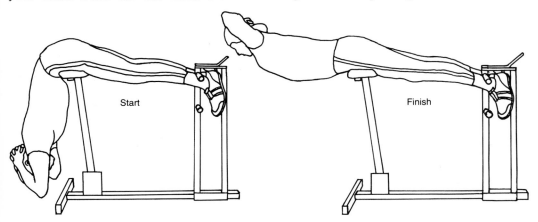

Fig 89 Back hyperextension.

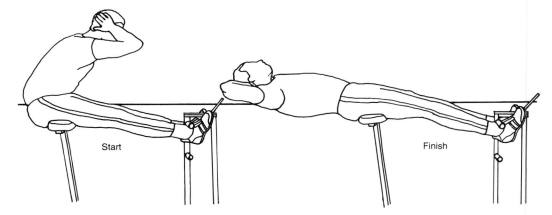

Fig 90 Extended sit-up.

which is worn with the shoulder straps tight to keep it firmly against the shoulders.

An exercise cycle that is fitted with a mechanism to increase the resistance is one of the most efficient methods of improving strength. Set the resistance so that it is difficult to move the pedals. At first complete four or five one-minute exercises with a 30–45-second rest between each. As it becomes increasingly easy to pedal, either increase the number of exercises or alternatively reduce the rest intervals. Ensure that the leg is fully straightened during the pedalling action.

Strengthening and improving the stability of the knee joint is vitally important. This can be achieved with the following simple exercise.

Sit on a chair wearing a ski boot or with some other additional load on the foot or ankle. Raise the leg to the horizontal. Bend the leg 20–25° and then return it to the horizontal. Repeat until extreme discomfort is felt in the muscles above the knee joint. Rest for 30–45 seconds. Repeat 8–10 times.

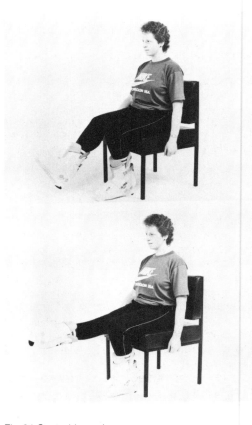

Fig 91 Seated leg raise.

72

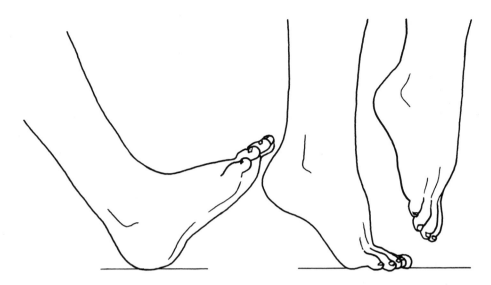

Fig 92 Full range of movement of the ankle joint.

POWER

To be entirely accurate, *power* should be defined using a formula that many will have forgotten from their school physics:

$$\text{Power} = \frac{\text{Force} \times \text{Distance}}{\text{Time}}$$

In simpler terms it may be described as a quick, strong movement where a joint is moved through its full range.

A recreational skier's technique is dependent on his or her ability to initiate turns by making simultaneous powerful movements of the ankle and knee joints. Only with this correct use of the two joints can exaggerated and unnecessary upper body movements, which cause a loss of balance and posture, be avoided.

Power is improved by creating a small overload of increased weight and concentrating on making the movements as quickly as possible. Body-weight is usually a suffi-

cient load, additional external weights are not necessary. The following exercises are designed to obtain an improvement in power. In all it is essential to ensure that the ankle joint is exercised through its full range of movement.

Skipping

Complete four or five exercises of 3–4 minutes duration, with a minute's rest between each set.

Running

Run in soft earth, sand or snow with an emphasis on speed over 40–50 metres. Complete 8–10 sprints with a recovery interval of 45–60 seconds between each sprint.

Fig 93 Skipping.

Fig 94 Ankle lifts.

Ankle Lifts

Stand with toes on the edge of a bench, chair or block of wood. Allow the heels to lower, then quickly lift to stretch height and lower again. Repeat as many as possible in 30 seconds. Allow a recovery of 45 seconds before repeating the exercise. Complete 6–8 exercises with the same recovery interval.

Box Jumps

The same box jumps as used in the fitness test provide a good conditioning exercise. Do as many as possible in 30 seconds. Allow a 45-second recovery interval, then repeat. Complete 6–8 exercises with an interval between each.

Hopping

Hop as fast as possible over 30–40 metres. Allow a recovery break of 30–45 seconds, then hop the same distance using the other leg. Repeat 8–10 times on each leg.

All trainees should aim to include at least one power training session a week, preferably two. A good training session that will create sufficient overload to obtain an improvement in power should last for at least 45 minutes. Include as many of the exercises as possible. In addition to the recovery period between each repetition of an exercise, a further 2–3 minutes recovery should be allowed between each exercise.

AGILITY, BALANCE, CONFIDENCE AND CO-ORDINATION

There is no evidence to suggest that 'off ski' exercises have any positive effect on a recreational skier's agility, balance, confidence or co-ordination. While in purist term these are facets of fitness, they are also an integral part of ski technique and adults can make the greatest improvement with task-specific practices on skis.

In most ski schools clients are asked to do some simple, general exercises that help to improve the four qualities. But because most of the ski teachers are working within the confines of a ski test system they tend to move on from these practices before they are learned and can have any lasting effect on the learning of skills.

The following group of exercises was devised by Alan Ashfield during his work with junior skiers. The exercises were so successful that Alan has now incorporated them into many of his adult classes at the Telford Ski Centre and has found that they are equally beneficial to skiers of all abilities and aspirations.

The key to their success lies in repeating them often enough for learning to take place and to influence performance.

Running in the fall-line, lift first one leg and then the other.

Sliding in the fall-line, make a running action.

Staying in the fall-line, step both skis to one side and then the other.

Hop lightly from both feet.

Staying in the fall-line and while retaining a snowplough shape, hop lightly.

While making snowplough turns lift the inside (non-steering) foot.

Make a series of long-radius turns whilst making a continuous stepping action.

Make a series of long-radius turns whilst making a continuous hopping action.

7 Mental Fitness

The physical attributes that make up fitness are vitally important in determining whether learning and performance are successful. However, all performance is dependent on each individual's mental approach to the task. It is the keystone that holds everything else in place. In order to achieve a high success rate it is necessary to be in the right frame of mind. A casual, laid-back attitude will cause a lowering of attainment, as will a tense, nervous approach.

The Yerkes–Dodson arousal curve best (Fig 95) illustrates the complicated relationship between a performer's mental state or arousal and his or her level of performance. The best results are achieved when one is approaching the top of the arousal curve at AB. A common phrase used to describe this condition is 'psyched up'. Being over-aroused is commonly called 'over the top'.

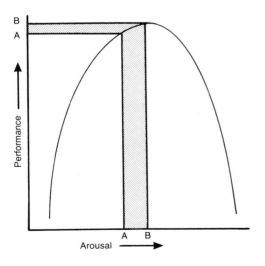

Fig 95 The Yerkes–Dodson arousal curve.

Failure to achieve the optimum arousal and performance may be due to only one or to a combination of the factors listed in Fig 96. Most are within the control of the individual skier, who must learn to recognise the problems and make the necessary adjustments in order to achieve improved performance.

It is possible, however, to give some guidance concerning one increasingly obvious problem area, which causes unnecessary anxiety and adversely affects the level of performance of many recreational skiers.

The participants in skiing more than any other sport or recreation seem to be motivated increasingly by egocentricity and the image they wish to project to others. It is an infectious malaise that places many under great pressure to succeed – and that, of course, is one sure way of ensuring that failure, not success, will be the end result.

There are those, for example, who misguidedly think that the length of the skis used gives some status or ability to the user. This is a dangerous myth. No one should allow themselves to be pressurised into using skis that reduce their confidence and arousal and, as a consequence, lower their achievement. Shorter skis are easier to turn, and as this is the essence of skiing there is no point in making it difficult to learn by wearing long skis in order to impress others.

The same is true of ski boots. There is no inherent merit in wearing high ski boots. They are appropriate only for the technical requirements of the racer and the best of the advanced skiers. Simply putting them on does not confer that technical status on the user. In fact it is more likely to affect adversely a recreational skier's technical ability because they are stiff and inhibit a

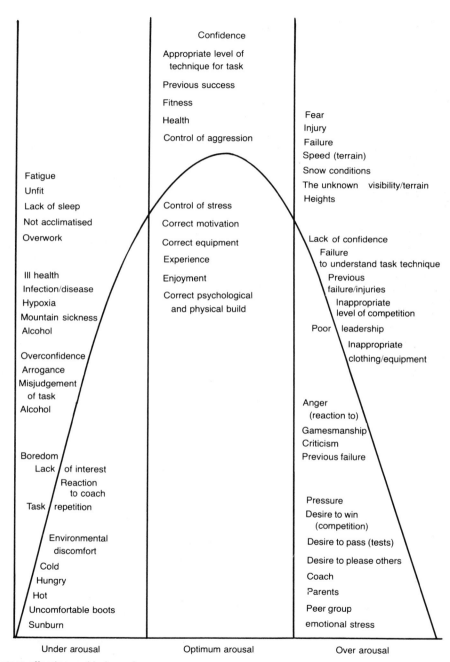

Fig 96 Factors affecting a skier's performance.

correct use of the ankle joint. The priorities in choosing boots are firstly comfort and secondly the ease of movement of the ankle through its normal range.

Increasingly, skiers wishing to raise their status associate where they have skied with their own and others' ability. Consequently, many are tempted to tackle pistes where the degree of difficulty is well beyond their technical ability in order that they can accord themselves a higher status in the hierarchy. It is a dangerous practice that contributes to the number of accidents. Those who literally only just survive without physical injury do little to improve their real ability. In fact, the experience is likely to have an adverse effect as what must amount to technical failure will impose stress on their mental attitude. Bad skiing interrupts the learning curve and causes a lowering of technical ability until confidence in one's real ability is restored. This comes from learning and practising on comparatively easy terrain where it is possible to concentrate on the movement patterns of the techniques and not be forced 'over the top' by the size of the moguls or the steepness of the terrain. Optimum arousal is more likely to be achieved if skiers concentrate on how they ski, not where they ski.

8 The Resort

Brochures, postcards, posters and even holiday snaps show ski resorts as idyllic places. They all create an illusion because ski resorts are perhaps the most dangerous of all the recreation arenas in which we play. The conditions necessary to give good skiing combine to form a most hostile environment. All emphasise the need to improve fitness prior to the visit and to exercise some control over life-style in the resort if the skiing is to be worthwhile.

ALTITUDE

Any increase in height above sea level causes a reduction in the pressure of oxygen in the air. In most ski resorts the increase in altitude is sufficient to affect significantly the volume of oxygen that is available as a fuel to the working organs and muscles. The most noticeable effect is that work capacity is reduced in terms of both output and duration. It is not possible to work as hard or as long at high altitudes as it is at lower altitudes. In addition, the recovery time following medium and heavy workloads is increased.

A reduction of oxygen in the tissues can also affect the parts of the brain that control co-ordination and judgement. The danger is that skiers affected in this way not only are unable to recognise a lower level of performance in themselves but, more seriously, may also think that their performance is more skilled than usual. This may well lead to overconfidence and result in accidents and injury.

There is some disagreement among exercise physiologists as to the critical height at which one would expect to notice this effect – it is, of course, dependent on each individual's tolerance to exposure to altitude – but 2,300 metres would seem to be the height at which those with a low tolerance would certainly be affected. Their susceptibility is increased by:

- exposure to the cold
- physical and mental fatigue
- alcohol

The effects of exposure to altitude are reduced in those persons with a good level of preparatory stamina. However, no one is immune and some acclimatisation is always necessary. It is aided if the workload is kept well below maximum for the first two days.

Exposure to altitude causes dehydration, which adversely affects health and physical fitness.

COLD

Bright sunlight sometimes tempts the foolhardy to leave the hotel inadequately dressed for protection against the dangers associated with the low temperatures experienced in all ski resorts.

Frostbite

The skin is kept warm by the blood. When the external temperature is low, blood flow is restricted to the extremities – the hands, feet, nose and ears – to avoid excessive heat loss. When the skin becomes very cold, blood circulation stops and the water between the skin and the blood capillaries is turned to ice. This is termed 'frostbite'.

The incidence of frostbite is reduced by

wearing the correct clothing. Gloves or mittens, warm socks and a hat will protect the hands, feet and ears. In extremely low temperatures, a scarf will afford some protection to the lips, nose and cheeks.

Accidental Hypothermia

The temperature of the human body is maintained at 98.4 °F (37 °C). It is regulated by a complex system that balances the heat generated by the active tissues against the heat lost to the environment. Prolonged exposure to the cold can result in a severe chilling of the body surface. When this heat loss continues to exceed heat gain, chilling of the body core and of vital organs will result.

The incidence can be reduced only if the heat loss is controlled by wearing clothing suited for use in the activity. It creates a controllable microclimate, insulating the body from the cold by trapping layers of warm air between the layers of clothing. For this reason it is preferable to wear three or four layers of comparatively thin clothing rather than two thick ones. It gives better insulation and greater flexibility in warmer weather or when the work rate is high. Ski clothing should not absorb moisture as the loss of body heat is increased by as much as 90 per cent when the clothing is wet. It is essential for safety, therefore, to wear clothing designed and proven to be suitable rather than to adapt other garments or to wear clothing such as denim jeans that is totally unsuitable and dangerous.

Ski clothing should also be windproof. It is possible for severe chilling to occur in comparatively high temperatures if there is a strong wind.

While the cold is the primary cause of accidental hypothermia, the following may also be contributory factors:

- exhaustion from overexertion
- low energy reserves due to inadequate food consumption
- alcohol
- dehydration
- shock following an accident

Warm-Up

Not all the time spent on the mountain is active. Some stops are unavoidable, such as waiting in queues for transport up the mountain. Some are voluntary, such as resting and taking refreshment. All may cause warm muscles to cool, stiffen and become less responsive during the first run after a break. A few warm-up exercises can easily return the muscles to working temperature.

ULTRAVIOLET RADIATION

The most obvious environmental hazard to a skier is the harmful effect of ultraviolet radiation. Two factors contribute to an increase in its intensity. Firstly, the mountain air is free from dust, water vapour and pollutants, which at a lower altitude act as a filter and prevent some of the sun's rays from reaching the ground. Secondly, the snow reflects 90 per cent of the potentially harmful rays. Even on cloudy days the danger is higher than one might expect. Ultraviolet light, having penetrated the cloud cover, is reflected and re-reflected between the cloud base and the snow.

All too frequently carelessness and an overanxiety to obtain the status symbol suntan are the causes of many skiers becoming sunburnt – a condition that can in severe cases result in them having to stay indoors for a number of days.

A suntan is the body's defence mechanism against sunburn. Until the tan is well established it is essential to protect the skin by the application of screening lotions and barrier creams. Care must be taken to ensure that all exposed areas – under the chin, on the neck and behind the ears, not forgetting the ears themselves – are covered.

Fig 97 Leg lifts.

Fig 98 Hopping.

The eyes are very sensitive to ultraviolet light. Prolonged exposure at altitude causes mere discomfort at first, followed by snow blindness. It can be prevented only by wearing sunglasses or goggles.

One of the most unpleasant and painful effects of exposure to the sun and the cold is the swelling and cracking of the lips. This, too, can be avoided by applying screening and barrier creams. The herpes virus is activated by ultraviolet light. Sufferers can minimise the likelihood of problems by applying a barrier cream.

ALCOHOL

Shakespeare was not referring to skiers when in *Macbeth* he wrote of alcohol, 'It provokes the desire, but it takes away the performance.' Nevertheless it is true; drinking alcohol probably contributes more to skiers' poor performance and accidents than any other environmental factor.

No doubt concerned by the quite appalling number of skiing accidents, researchers at Innsbruck University investigated the correlation between the number of accidents and the consumption of alcohol. In the survey, 25 per cent of the accidents investigated were found to be alcohol related.

Alcohol acts on the brain as an anaesthetic. Under its influence those functions of the

Fig 99 Hamstring stretch.

Fig 100 The forward-backward splits.

brain that safeguard man – judgement and control – are the first to be impaired.

Dr Mebbelinde has shown a deterioration in micromuscular performance even after the consumption of a small quantity of alcohol. With a blood alcohol concentration of 30mg/100ml, the equivalent of one pint of beer, the following deterioration was noted:

- a 10 per cent decrease in speed over 80 metres
- a 6 per cent decrease in power in the sargent jump test
- great deterioration in balance and posture control

But perhaps the most convincing statistics relate to driving a motor vehicle. With a

Fig 101 Stretching the inner thigh.

84

Fig 102 Snowplough hops.

blood alcohol concentration of 50mg/100ml accident proneness is increased by 50 per cent, with 60mg/100ml accidents are doubled, with 80mg/100ml accidents are quadrupled, and with 150mg/100ml accidents increase 25 times. Because alcohol is retained in the blood for a long period, it is possible in the UK to be 'over the limit' and deemed unsafe to drive the morning after high intake. Yet many skiers expect to learn and perform the techniques of a very difficult sport with blood alcohol levels that would most certainly result in a driving ban.

In addition to its harmful effects on human performance, alcohol can also accentuate the effects of the cold environment. It causes a mild degree of tissue dehydration. It also increases the metabolic heat load and interferes with a physiological mechanism important in the control of body temperature. A flushing of the skin relieves the unpleasant sensation of feeling cold, but it is an illusion fraught with danger as alcohol actually accelerates the lowering of body temperature.

It would be both naïve and pointless to suggest that all skiers should not drink alcohol. However, what is obvious and sensible is to suggest that those who ski must make a very clear choice between, on the one hand, learning the techniques of the sport correctly and being able to perform them skilfully and, on the other, finding learning extremely difficult and allowing their performance to deteriorate to such a low level that they are a danger to themselves and everyone who is unfortunate enough to be near them on a ski piste.

If skiing well is a priority then clearly alcohol intake must be restricted to not more than a glass or two during the day. Après-ski consumption should be low enough to guarantee being well within the legal, 'safe' driving limit before skiing the next day.

FATIGUE

Tiredness makes learning and performance difficult. The energy requirement of a week's skiing holiday can, when all the

85

allied activities are included, be the equivalent of swimming the Channel. It is not surprising, then, that some find this excessive and are forced to limit the time spent on the mountain. While stamina training will improve staying power, it cannot be expected to endow those with a passion for the 'high life' with superhuman qualities. In order to survive a week's or a fortnight's skiing, common sense must be applied to planning a programme.

First and most obvious, adequate rest and sleep is essential to aid recovery from the exertions of both the skiing and the après skiing.

Secondly, not so obvious but equally important, it is absolutely essential to ensure that the massive energy output is compensated for by 'taking on' an equal amount of fuel or food. Sufficient supplies of foods rich in carbohydrates are the key for everyone,

weight watchers included, because they are the food most easily broken down to provide a source of energy. Bread, potatoes and pastas in all forms should be high on the list of requirements.

SKIING ACCIDENTS

It is not sensible to consider the objective hazards of ski resorts without including some reference to skiing accidents, their causes and, most importantly, the ways in which they may be reduced.

It is an unfortunate fact that skiers are more likely to suffer an injury that requires medical attention than the participants in all other hazardous outdoor pursuits. There are an estimated 200,000 such accidents in the Alps every year. Fortunately, however, the risk of a fatal accident is lower in skiing.

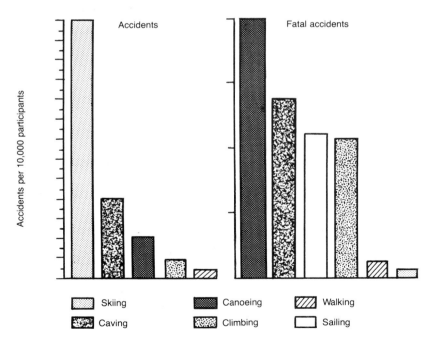

Fig 103 A comparison of the number of accidents in skiing and other sports.

Extensive research in Austria, Japan, Sweden and West Germany has identified the following as being the most common causes.

Alcohol

The detrimental effect of alcohol and its contribution to the cause of skiing accidents has already been mentioned. Clearly, if the estimate that it is the single most important cause in 25 per cent of all accidents is correct, only a dramatic change in behaviour patterns can bring about an improvement.

Lack of Fitness

Without preparatory fitness training, the techniques of the sport may be learned incorrectly. The resultant unskilled performance causes many accidents because the skiers do not have the ability to control themselves sufficiently to be safe. Fatigue can cause even skilled performance to deteriorate, and when it does the likelihood of an accident increases.

Unsuitable Equipment and Clothing

This category includes all those accidents caused by using skis that are too long for the user's technical ability and ski boots that are too high and stiff, and therefore place an unnecessary loading on the bones of the lower leg and the knee joint when the binding does not open in a twisting fall. It is unlikely that the bindings used by most adults would be deemed unsuitable. All modern bindings will work if they are maintained well and set correctly. However, it is not unusual for children to use bindings that are designed for adults. Because the children are too light and too weak, the bindings do not work and injury results.

An improvement will be achieved only by individuals making a wiser and more informed choice when they purchase their own equipment. Those who hire the equipment as part of the tour operator's package need to be rather more discerning in what they will accept. Similarly, the tour operators themselves need to make improvements in the standard of some of the equipment provided for their clients.

Unsuitable clothing that causes the wearer to become wet and cold is a primary cause of some accidents. It is absolutely essential to ensure that any clothing purchased will fulfil its intended function and insulate and protect the wearer from the very hostile environment. It is worth remembering that there is a great deal of truth in the old adage, 'You get what you pay for.'

Poor Maintenance of Equipment

Skiing on poorly maintained equipment may be compared to driving a car that has failed its MOT test. Quite simply, it is unlikely to do what the 'driver' wants or what the manufacturer had designed it to do.

Again there is a duality of responsibility. Those who own their own equipment must service it before their holiday and as required during their stay. This includes waxing as necessary, sharpening the edges and ensuring that the bindings are in working order. They can, for example, ice up if they are left in the shade during a stop for refreshments and rest.

Similarly, those who provide equipment for hire must make every effort to give the clients well-maintained skis.

Overestimation of Ski Ability

In most hazardous activities it is the exception rather than the rule to find participants attempting tasks that are not in keeping with their technical ability. Novice canoeists avoid Grade 4 water, novice and inexperienced rock climbers do not attempt to lead very severe routes, and inexperienced helmsmen do not enter the Fastnet race. In marked and frightening contrast, in every ski resort both novice and inexperienced skiers are seen on pistes far beyond their ability. Not surprisingly, they are much more likely to be involved in a serious accident than more competent skiers.

The frequency of such accidents can be reduced only by each individual adopting a more realistic approach to his or her own ability. Similarly. those who encourage inexperienced skiers to place themselves at risk must reflect on the possible outcome of their actions. It is, of course, understandable that friends of differing abilities will want to ski together. However, the onus is clearly on the better skiers to stay on pistes that are well within the capabilities of the others.

Inability to Assess Snow and Weather Conditions

Mountaincraft is a skill that many associate only with hill walking and rock climbing in the British mountains and with expeditions in the Alps, Himalayas and other major mountain ranges. However, it should be just as much part of a skier's repertoire of skills if he or she wants to move around the mountains in winter in comparative safety.

Learning to recognise the possible threats to one's safety posed by the ever-changing snow and weather conditions is not an easy task. It comes only after considerable experience gained with local experts. The possibility of accidents is reduced by being in the right place at the right time.

Failure to Observe the Rules of the Piste

Skiers, like motorists, are in part dependent on others for their safety. Just as sensible motorists must conform to the *Highway Code* if they are not to be a constant danger to themselves and others, so skiers must conform to the Ski Code.

Failure to Observe Notices

The notices which are placed at strategic places in a ski resort to warn of avalanche danger and piste closure for a number of reasons are there to protect skiers from known or potential danger. Those who ignore their advice openly court danger and place life and limb at risk – not only for themselves and their companions but also those who must, if necessary, rescue and evacuate them.

9 Cross-Country Skiing

Soccer and rugby originate from a common source. Both are played on a grass pitch and have the word 'football' in their official titles. But there any real similarity ends. The rules, the shape of the ball and goals are different. One is played mainly with the hands, the other with the feet; even the numbers in a team are different.

The same is true of alpine and nordic skiing. Both have a common playing surface and origin. But like the two codes of football, they have diverged so much in their equipment and technique that they must be considered as completely different in terms of their fitness requirements.

The key difference between the two is shown by comparing the maximum oxygen uptake capacity and percentage of slow twitch muscle fibre (Fig 104). These two physical qualities determine a person's stamina and muscular endurance. Good cross-country skiers are similar to long-distance runners in terms of their requirement, while alpine skiers are similar to ice-hockey players and sprinters. Further differences are shown by a full profile of nordic skiing (Fig 105).

Stamina and muscular endurance are without doubt the key factors and determine the recreational skier's level of attainment and enjoyment of the sport. Without these two physical qualities, anyone attempting even quite a short distance on a cross-country skiing track will find the effort quite a stressful experience. Cross-country skiing, unlike its alpine cousin, is almost entirely dependent on the participants' muscular efforts. They do not even have the luxury of mechanical uphill transport. Alpine skiers utilise gravity as the source of power, with the legs doing the bulk of the work. Cross-country participants are reliant on their legs and their arms to move them.

Mobility must be considered important. Firstly, it permits the correct pattern of movement at the hips and shoulders. Moreover, it reduces the incidence and severity of muscle stiffness and soreness which is very frequently associated with the workloads imposed by nordic skiing, just as it can be by cross-country running.

Power is an important facet of physical preparation if the technique is to be correct. Forward movement is obtained from the combined powerful use of arms and legs.

Strength is a low priority in the preparation. Participants are not subjected to the stress of high-speed turns and, as the heel is not fixed to the ski by a rigid binding, serious injury is much less common than it is in alpine skiing. As the forces are also much less, safety is not dependent on the ability to hold the leg rigid in a fall. The prevention of injury depends more on mobility than on strength.

The Group B facets of fitness, which were considered to be an integral part of alpine technique, all contribute to a nordic skier's ability. Again it is best to develop these qualities on skis as it is most unlikely that any positive and beneficial transfer of training will occur from exercises that are done without skis on.

THE TRAINING PROGRAMME

In order that participants are able to plan and evaluate the effectiveness of their training programme, it is necessary to determine their level of fitness at the outset by testing.

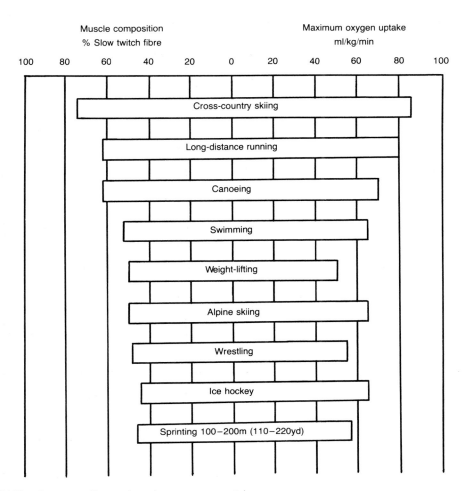

Muscle composition
% Slow twitch fibre

Maximum oxygen uptake
ml/kg/min

100 80 60 40 20 0 20 40 60 80 100

Cross-country skiing

Long-distance running

Canoeing

Swimming

Weight-lifting

Alpine skiing

Wrestling

Ice hockey

Sprinting 100–200m (110–220yd)

Fig 104 Muscle composition and maximum oxygen uptake.

Testing Current Fitness

Mobility

Use test Mobility 1 and 2 from Chapter 2. In addition, the following tests the mobility of the shoulder girdle in the plane of movement of the arms during the cross-country poling action.

Sit on the floor, legs bent and feet flat on the floor. Place the hands behind with the fingers pointing backwards. Lift the seat up and move forwards as far as possible. Measure the distance of the shoulders from the floor. This exercise may also be used to improve mobility of the shoulders. (Fig 106.)

Stamina/Muscular Endurance

The 12-minute stamina test utilised in Chapter 2 is the preferred test.

Power

Utilise the sargent jump test from Chapter 2.

90

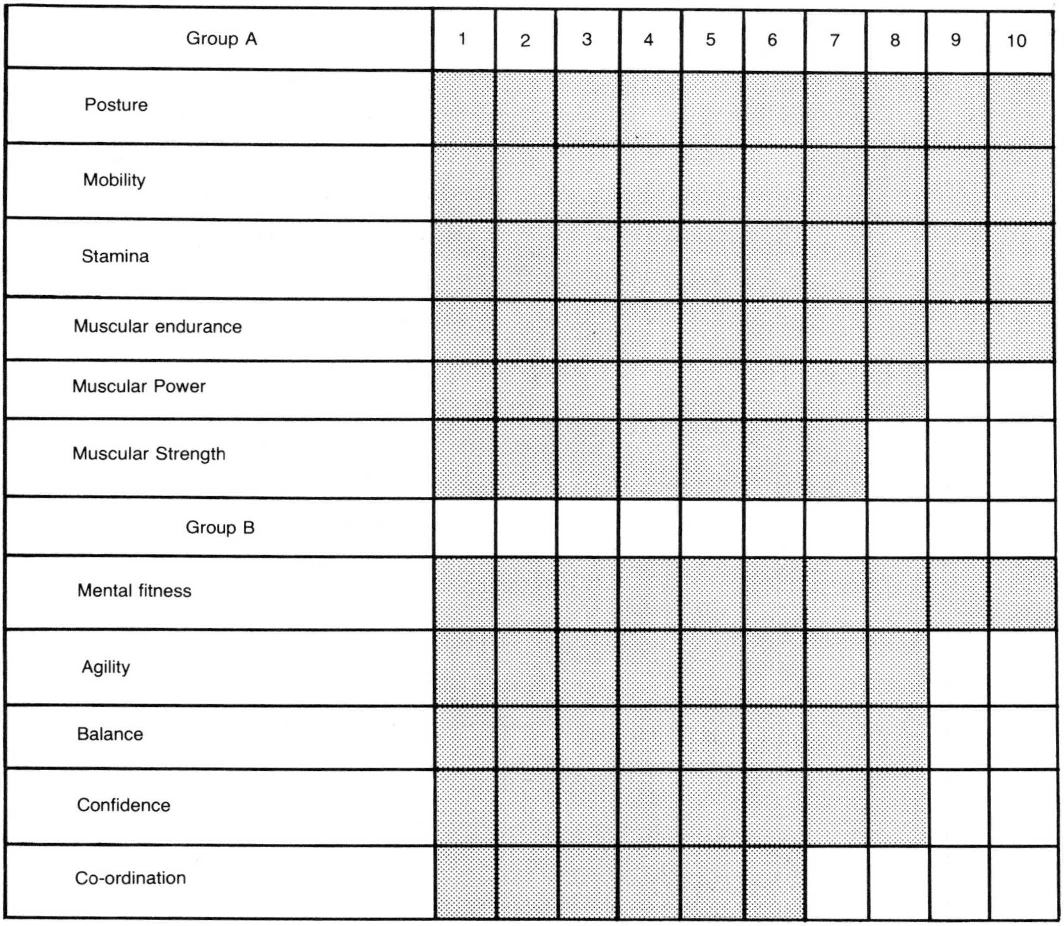

Group A	1	2	3	4	5	6	7	8	9	10
Posture										
Mobility										
Stamina										
Muscular endurance										
Muscular Power										
Muscular Strength										
Group B										
Mental fitness										
Agility										
Balance										
Confidence										
Co-ordination										

Fig 105 Cross-country skiing profile.

The scores obtained may also be taken from Fig 9 to indicate current fitness levels.

Planning a Programme

Determine how much time can be regularly devoted to training each week. Allocate this time to stamina/muscular endurance, mobility and power on the following basis:

Stamina/muscular endurance   3/5
Mobility   1/5
Power   1/5

If, for example, there are five hours available each week, three hours must be given to the most important aspect.

Stamina Training

The points system described in Chapter 5 may be used by cross-country enthusiasts. However, in view of the much heavier demands of cross-country skiing, it is necessary to set higher weekly targets during training in order that the preparation is more appropriate (see Fig 107).

Fig 106 Shoulder mobility.

Test Score	Age			
	Under 20	20–30	30–40	Over 40
5	45+	45	35–45	30
4	45+	35–45	30–35	25–30
3	35+	35	25–30	20–25
2	25+	20–25	15–20	15
1	20+	15+	15+	10–15
0	15	15	10	10

Fig 107

Real enthusiasts may find that the best training is provided by roller skis, on which they are able to use exactly the same movement pattern and muscular groups as they do on snow skis. Those using this training method

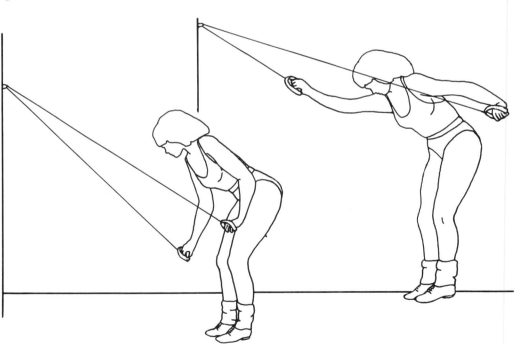

Fig 108.

Fig 109 Summer training.

should allocate 4 points per mile to the activity.

Mobility

Mobility training should follow that detailed in Chapter 3 and also include the shoulder girdle exercise from this chapter.

Power

Power is best improved with weight training for adults and circuit training for adoles- cents. The following exercise should also be added to the programme in order to im- prove the specific fitness of the shoulders and arms.

Thread either elasticated or ordinary ropes with a 5 kg weight attached through a retain- ing hook or pulley system 2.5–3 metres above the ground. Stand facing the wall with a rope in each hand. Lean forward from the waist. Alternate the pulls with the right and left arm.

Index

Index